Warrior • 71

Roman Legionary

58 BC–AD 69

Ross Cowan • Illustrated by Angus McBride

First published in Great Britain in 2003 by Osprey Publishing,
PO Box 883, Oxford, OX1 9PL, UK
PO Box 3985, New York, NY 10185-3985, USA
Email: info@ospreypublishing.com

Osprey Publishing is part of the Osprey Group.

A CIP catalogue record for this book is available from the British Library

ISBN: 978 1 84176 600 3

Editorial by Tom Lowres
Design by Ken Vail Graphic Design, Cambridge, UK
Index by Alan Thatcher
Typeset in Helvetica Neue and ITC New Baskerville
Originated by Grasmere Digital Imaging, Leeds, UK
Printed in China through World Print Ltd.

14 15 16 17 18   24 23 22 21 20 19 18 17 16 15 14 13

The Woodland Trust
Osprey Publishing is supporting the Woodland Trust, the UK's leading
woodland conservation charity, by funding the dedication of trees.

www.ospreypublishing.com

Artist's note

Readers may care to note that the original paintings from
which the colour plates in this book were prepared are
available for private sale. All reproduction copyright
whatsoever is retained by the Publishers. All enquiries
should be addressed to:

> Scorpio
> 158 Mill Road
> Hailsham, East Sussex
> BN27 2SH
> UK
>
> Email: scorpiopaintings@btinternet.com

The Publishers regret that they can enter into no
correspondence upon this matter.

Author's acknowledgements

Special thanks to the Cowan family, Donal Bateson, Duncan
Campbell, Brian Cowan, Rebecca Cullen, Colin Cumming,
Eckhard Deschler-Erb, Lawrence Keppie, Tom Lowres,
Thomas McGrory, Jennifer Murray, Steven D. P. Richardson,
Dimos Spatharas, Krista Ubbels, Susanne Wilbers-Rost
and Holly Young. Thanks also to the Hunterian Museum
at the University of Glasgow; Landesmuseum Bonn;
Landesmuseum Mainz; Varusschlacht im Osnabrücker
Land – Museum und Park Kalkriese.

Author's note

Translated quotes are adapted from the Loeb Classical
Library unless otherwise stated.

CONTENTS

ROMAN LEGIONARY 58 BC–AD 69

INTRODUCTION

In 58 BC Julius Caesar embarked on his conquest of Gaul, an aggressive and ultimately unsanctioned venture that caused the fragile constitution of Republican Rome to collapse. When Caesar's tenure as a provincial governor ended in 49 BC, he was expected to disband his legions and return to Rome to face trial. Instead he chose war. He crossed the Rubicon into Italy and marched on Rome, had himself made *dictator* (an emergency magistracy concentrating power in his hands) and defeated his opponents in the Balkans, Egypt, Asia Minor, North Africa and Spain. In 44 BC he was made *dictator* for life and prepared to march against Parthia, but was assassinated by the Liberators led by Brutus and Cassius. In 43 BC the Caesarian factions headed by Mark Antony, legate of Caesar, and Octavian, adopted son and heir of Caesar, clashed in battle. However, at the close of the year Antony, Octavian and a third commander, Lepidus, united to form a special board of three, a triumvirate, to concentrate power in their hands and eradicate their opponents. Anyone voicing opposition to the triumvirs' almost regal powers was removed: thus old republicans like Cicero were executed and Brutus and Cassius, who were still alive and stood for the restoration of the old Republic, were defeated and killed at the battle of Philippi in 42 BC. But intense friction remained between Antony and Octavian. Lepidus was eased out of power, and by 40 BC the Roman world was effectively divided into eastern and western halves held by Antony and Octavian. A final conflict for total control was inevitable and in 31 BC the unlikely Octavian triumphed over the charismatic Antony and his lover Cleopatra at the battle of Actium. Octavian pursued the despairing Antony to Egypt, forcing him to commit suicide. In 30 BC the civil war finally ended.

Octavian remodelled the army into a permanent force of 28 legions and instigated the greatest period of Roman expansion. Recognised as the first emperor and renamed Augustus (he reigned between 27 BC and AD 14), his legions conquered northern Spain, all Europe south of the River Danube, and Germany west of the River Elbe. The Illyrian revolt of AD 6–9 and the destruction of three legions in Germany in AD 9 caused the expansionist policy to falter, but in AD 43 the Emperor Claudius began the conquest of Britain. Further major conquests (e.g. in Germany, Dacia, Mesopotamia) then occurred every generation or so. However, the most serious wars of the Empire were

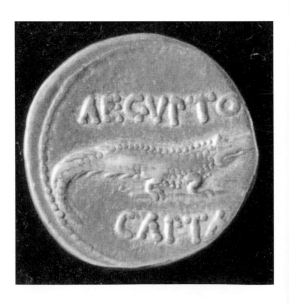

Denarius issued under Octavian, 28 BC, celebrating the conquest of Egypt in 30 BC. (Hunter Coin Cabinet, University of Glasgow)

often those of Roman against Roman. The Imperial legions were as susceptible to revolt as their late Republican predecessors, as occurred in AD 68–70. This book examines the legionaries who took part in these conquests and civil wars and seeks to understand how they won (and lost) their battles.

CHRONOLOGY

BC

60 First Triumvirate – coalition of Caesar, Pompey and Crassus dominates Roman politics

58–51 Caesar's conquest of Gaul; British and German expeditions

53 Crassus defeated and killed by Parthians at Carrhae (south-east Turkey); Cassius leads remnants of army to safety

49 Caesar crosses the River Rubicon into Italy; civil war with Pompey

48 Pompey repels Caesar at Dyrrachium; Caesar victorious at Pharsalus (Greece)

47 Pompey murdered; Caesar in Alexandria; Caesar defeats Pharnaces at Zela (Turkey)

46 Caesar defeats Pompeians at Thapsus (North Africa)

45 Caesar defeats Pompeians at Munda (Spain)

44 Caesar assassinated in Rome by 'Liberators' led by Brutus and Cassius (15 March); Octavian arrives in Italy; discord with Antony

43 Antony defeated at Forum Gallorum and Mutina (Italy); Antony, Octavian and Lepidus reconciled (Second Triumvirate); Sextus Pompeius, son of Pompey, seizes Sicily

42 Sextus Pompeius intercepts triumviral transports in Adriatic, legio Martia destroyed; Antony victorious over Brutus and Cassius at Philippi (Macedonia)

41 Antony in east; quarrels with Octavian; Antony's brother, L. Antonius, besieged by Octavian at Perusia (Italy)

40 Surrender of L. Antonius; Antony attacks Brundisium (Italy); Antony and Octavian reconciled; Parthians invade Syria while Labienus, Caesar's former legate, attacks Asia Minor

39–38 Ventidius Bassus, legate of Antony, defeats Labienus and Parthians

36 Sextus Pompeius' fleet defeated at Naucholus (Sicily) by Agrippa for Octavian

36 Antony's Parthian expedition fails

31 Octavian and Agrippa defeat Antony and Cleopatra at Actium

30 Octavian invades Egypt; deaths of Antony and Cleopatra; reorganisation of legions

29–27 Crassus (grandson of the Triumvir) expands Roman territory north of Macedonia to Danube

27 Octavian becomes Augustus, effectively emperor

27–19 Conquest of north-west Spain

25 Galatia annexed, legio XXII Deiotariana enters Roman Army

25–24 Arabia Felix (Aden) expedition fails

24–22 Expedition to Ethiopia

20 Standards captured from Crassus and Antony returned by the Parthians

17–16 Sugambri invade Gaul; legio V Alaudae loses eagle

16–14 Drusus and Tiberius conquer Alps, Raetia and Noricum

13–9 Drusus campaigns in Germany; Romans reach the River Elbe; death of Drusus (9 BC)

6 BC–AD 2 Tiberius in exile

AD

4–5 Resumption of German operations

6–9 Illyrian revolt

9 Varus' army of three legions (XVII, XVIII, XIX) and nine auxiliary units annihilated in Teutoburg Forest by Cherusci; Tiberius secures the Rhine

14 Death of Augustus; accession of Tiberius; Lower German and Pannonian legions mutiny

14–16 Germanicus' German expeditions; Arminius defeated at Idistaviso (AD 16), recovery of two eagles lost in AD 9

17 Cappadocia annexed

18–23 Revolt of Tacfarinas in Africa

21 Revolt of Florus and Sacrovir in Gaul

28 Frisian revolt

39 Caligula's operations in Germany and Gaul

41 Caligula assassinated; Claudius becomes emperor; Galba defeats Chatti; Gabinius defeats Chauci, recovering third eagle lost in AD 9

41–42 Paulinus subdues Mauretania; Mauretania organised as province (AD 44)

42 Revolt of Scribonianus in Dalmatia

43 Invasion of Britain

46 Thrace annexed

47 Eastern Pontus annexed; Corbulo campaigns against Cherusci; Frisii subdued

54 Claudius poisoned; Nero becomes emperor

58–63 Corbulo's Armenian campaigns

58–61 Paulinus advances frontier in Britain; revolt of Boudicca (AD 60–61)

66–72 Jewish revolt; Vespasian and Titus campaign in Judaea (AD 67–69)

68 Revolt of Vindex in Gaul; Nero overthrown; Galba becomes emperor

69 Year of the Four Emperors: Galba murdered by praetorians in Rome; Otho succeeds, supported by praetorians and new legions I and II Adiutrix; Otho defeated by Vitellius, governor of Lower Germany, at First Cremona; Vespasian proclaimed emperor by army of Syria; his forces (Flavians) defeat Vitellians at Second Cremona; revolt of Civilis and Batavi. Rome falls to the Flavians

70 Titus captures Jerusalem; Civilis defeated

The Augustan Legions (see Keppie 1984: 132–44, 205–13)

Legion and final title	Formed by	Meaning / purpose of title	Emblem
I Germanica	Caesar in 48 or Vibius Pansa in 43; with Octavian from 41 BC	For service in Germany	Unknown
II Augusta	Pansa in 43? With Octavian from 41 BC	Reconstituted by Augustus	Capricorn, zodiac sign favoured by Augustus, indicative of reconstitution, and Pegasus
III Augusta	Pansa in 43 or Octavian in 41–40 BC	Reconstituted by Augustus	Pegasus?
III Cyrenaica	Lepidus in 40–36, or Antony before 31 BC	For battle honours in Cyrenaica (Libya)	Unknown
III Gallica	Caesar in 48, with Antony from 40 BC	Service in Gaul, 48–42 BC	Bull – Caesarian origin
IIII Macedonica	Caesar in 48; defects from Antony to Octavian in 43 BC	Service in Macedonia, 47–44 BC	Bull – Caesarian origin
IIII Scythica	Antony before 31 BC	Perhaps for victories in Scythia (Northern Balkans, Bulgaria), 29–27 BC	Capricorn – Augustan reconstitution
V Alaudae	Caesar in 52 from Gauls; with Antony 40–31 BC	'Larks' – after helmet crest	Elephant – victory over war elephants at Thapsus, 46 BC
V Macedonica	Pansa in 43 or Octavian 41–40 BC	Service in Macedonia after Actium	Bull, but not Caesarian
VI Ferrata	Caesar in 52; with Antony 43–31 BC	'Ironclad'	Romulus and Remus and she-wolf
VI Victrix	Octavian, 41–40 BC	'Victorious'	Bull?
VII Claudia	59 or earlier; with Caesar from 58; with Octavian from 44 BC	'Claudian' – for loyalty to Claudius during Scribonianus' revolt, AD 42	Bull – Caesarian origin
VIII Augusta	59 or earlier; with Caesar from 58; with Octavian from 44 BC	Reconstituted by Augustus	Bull – Caesarian origin
IX Hispana	Uncertain, perhaps Octavian, 41–40 BC	'Spanish', from service in Spain	Unknown
X Fretensis	Octavian 41–40 BC	For naval service in the *Fretum Siculum* channel between Italy and Sicily in 36 BC	Bull, dolphin, galley and boar
X Gemina	59 or earlier; with Caesar from 58; with Octavian from 44 BC	'Twin' – amalgamation of Caesar's X Equestris ('mounted') with another unit	Bull – Caesarian origin
XI Claudia	Uncertain, perhaps Octavian, 41–40 BC	'Claudian' – for loyalty to Claudius during Scribonianus' revolt, AD 42	Neptune
XII Fulminata	Caesar in 58; with Antony 43/2–31 BC	'Armed with lightning'	Thunderbolt
XIII Gemina	Uncertain, perhaps Octavian, 41–40 BC	'Twin' – amalgamation after Actium	Lion, symbol of Jupiter
XIV Gemina	Uncertain, perhaps Octavian, 41–40 BC	'Twin' – amalgamation after Actium	Capricorn – indicating reconstitution under Augustus
XV Apollinaris	Octavian, 41–40 BC?	'Sacred to Apollo', honouring the god to whom victory at Actium was attributed	Unknown
XVI Gallica, then Flavia Firma	Octavian, 41–40 BC?	For service in Gaul; 'Flavian and steadfast' after reformation, c.AD 70	Lion, symbol of Jupiter
XVII	Octavian, 41–40 BC?	-	Unknown
XVIII	Octavian, 41–40 BC?	-	Unknown
XIX	Octavian, 41–40 BC?	-	Unknown
XX Valeria Victrix	Octavian, 41–40 BC, or after Actium?	'Valiant, Victorious', for victory over Boudicca, AD 61	Boar
XXI Rapax	Octavian, 41–40 BC, or after Actium?	'Rapacious'	Capricorn – indicating Augustan origin/reconstitution
XXII Deiotariana	Formed from soldiers transferred to Roman Army at time of annexation of Galatia, 25 BC	After King Deiotarus of Galatia	Unknown

THE ESTABLISHMENT OF THE IMPERIAL LEGIONS

Following his victory at Actium in 31 BC and his conquest of Egypt in 30 BC, Octavian found perhaps 60 legions under his control. He immediately began a massive settlement programme for time-served veterans, and over the period of seven years whittled down the number of legions to 28, retaining especially the units raised by Julius Caesar and, as a symbol of unity, the most renowned of Antony's legions. Where before legions had been raised for specific wars and disbanded after six years, these 28 legions were permanent formations composed of long-service professionals (Suetonius, *Augustus* 49). As Augustus, he was the first leader to lay down clear terms of service, rates of pay and pensions for the successful completion of service. The chaos of the late Republican period was not to be repeated. The legions were no longer a citizen militia; no one but Augustus had the right to raise new legions and they depended upon him for their pay and owed their loyalty to him alone.

ORGANISATION, SIZE AND COMMAND OF THE LEGION

> *In a legion there are sixty centuries, thirty maniples, [and] ten cohorts.*
> Cincius Alimentus, quoted by Aulus Gellius, *Attic Nights*, 16.4.6.

The legion

A legion was composed of 60 centuries. Each century contained 80 soldiers and was commanded by a centurion. The essential under-officers of the century were, in order of seniority, the *signifer* (standard-bearer), *optio* (centurion's deputy) and *cornicen* or *bucinator* (trumpeter) and *tesserarius* (officer of the watchword). Six centuries formed a cohort. There were ten cohorts per legion, each 480 men strong, making the legion 4,800 infantry soldiers at maximum strength, but units were often under strength. The cavalry of the legion, numbering 120 in the AD 60s, was carried on the books of the centuries but formed their own corps during war (Pseudo-Hyginus, *De munitionibus castrorum*, 1, 7, 8, 30; Josephus, *Jewish War*, 3.120).

From 13 BC until the middle of the 1st century AD the veterans (i.e. those who had served 16 years) were transferred to the *vexillum veteranorum* (veterans' unit) for a further four years of service. With a strength of about 500 men and its own officers and administration, it might be attached to the legion or perform independent duties (Tacitus, *Annals*, 1.44, 3.21).

The legion also had a large number of slaves (*calones*) attached to it, perhaps 120 per cohort, at least on campaign. These were trained for particular duties and some were armed and might defend the camp (Josephus, *Jewish War*, 3.69; Roth 1994: 351).

Centuries and centurions

The centuries were paired as *prior* (front) and *posterior* (rear), indicating their origin from maniples, and classed as *pili*, *principes* or *hastati*. Until

ABOVE TOP **Claudian sestertius commemorating the colony established at Patras in 30 BC for veterans of Antony's legions X (Caesar's Equestris = Augustus' Gemina) and XII (Fulminata). (Hunter Coin Cabinet, University of Glasgow)**

ABOVE MIDDLE **Mark Antony legionary denarius, 32–31 BC, honouring legio XII Antiqua (later XII Fulminata). (Hunter Coin Cabinet, University of Glasgow)**

ABOVE BOTTOM **Legionary denarius issued by Mark Antony, 32–31 BC, showing an *aquila* flanked by two centurial standards. The legio XVIII honoured is probably not the ancestor of the legion destroyed in AD 9. (Hunter Coin Cabinet, University of Glasgow)**

the late 2nd century BC the legion was composed of 30 maniples, each of 160 or 120 men and commanded by two centurions, one senior, the other junior. The senior centurion had overall command of the maniple (Polybius, 6.24). Therefore, the later *prior* centurion may have had seniority over the *posterior* centurion. *Pili* centurions seem to have been the most senior in the cohort (but they did not command it), followed by *principes* then by the *hastati*, but this was probably a difference of seniority rather than of actual rank. The only centurions of clear superior rank were the *primi ordines* (front rankers), the centurions of the first cohort. The most senior was the *primus pilus* (first spear/javelin), whose century contained the *aquilifer*, the senior standard-bearer who carried the eagle standard containing the *genius* (spirit) of the legion, which was crucial to unit identity and morale. Despite the status of the *primus pilus* there is no evidence that he had overall command of the first cohort.

Most centurions were promoted from the ranks, progressing through the grades in the century over a period of ten or more years. However, some centurions were men of the equestrian order who had received direct commissions. The equestrian order was later Republican and Imperial Rome's 'middle' or business class, but originally signified men whose wealth was sufficient to equip themselves as cavalrymen. Equestrians were superior in class to ordinary soldiers and could be promoted directly to centurionates (and higher ranks) without prior experience.

Senior officers

By the close of Augustus' reign the legion was normally commanded by a legate (*legatus*), a senatorial officer, except in the special case of Egypt where the two legions, III Cyrenaica and XXII Deiotariana, were commanded by equestrian prefects (*praefecti*). The legate had six tribunes as his aides. One was a young man from the senatorial order (*tribunus laticlavius*), who by virtue of his class was the legate's theoretical second-in-command, but was really present to watch and learn. The five other tribunes were experienced equestrian officers (*tribuni angusticlavii*) who had commanded an auxiliary cohort prior to this promotion. However, none of the tribunes held any fixed command over the cohorts or centuries; they were present to aid the legate who might employ them as temporary ad hoc commanders in the field. The real officer of importance below the legate was the *praefectus castrorum* (prefect of the camp), a former *primus pilus* who oversaw the running of the camp, particularly its logistics and medical facilities. He was also responsible for training and maintaining the legion's artillery (i.e. torsion catapults), and would assume command of the legion in the absence of the legate or senior tribune.

The century as the primary tactical unit

The cohort is traditionally viewed as the primary tactical unit of the legion. This is certainly the impression given by Caesar and Tacitus, who tell of formations and tactics based around the cohort. However, it has been suggested that the cohort could not function as a tactical unit because it had no commander or obvious standard of its own, leaving the century as the primary tactical unit (Isaac 1994). The centurion, therefore, was the crucial professional officer in the legion; there was no permanent commander of a sub-unit of the legion greater in size than the century between him and the legate, whose tenure of command might be limited to only three years or so. The centuries were the primary tactical units of the legion, which was itself a mass administrative unit. When Caesar and Tacitus speak of cohorts moving in battle we should view them as groupings of centuries fighting in support of each other.

ENLISTMENT

Five hundred thousand Roman citizens swore the military oath to me.
(Augustus, *Res Gestae*, 3)

Age
Traditionally all Roman male citizens between the ages of 17 and 46 were liable for military service (Aulus Gellius, *Attic Nights* 10.28.1). Most recruits to the legions were aged between 17 and 23, with the peak age of enlistment being 20, but recruits as young as 13 and 14, and as old as 36 are known (Scheidel 1996: 99ff).

Background
The majority of legionaries claimed origin (*origo*) in a town or city, but few actually came from urban centres. Most cities were centres of agricultural trade and had substantial rural territories attached to them. Some parts of the Empire were particularly devoid of urbanisation and in many cases *origines* were simply spurious, granted at enlistment with Roman citizenship. Peasant farmers had been the backbone of the citizen militia of the Republic and the country remained the favoured source of recruits under the late Empire. Recruits with rural/agricultural backgrounds were preferred for their endurance and because they were unaffected by the sleazier distractions of city life:

> They are nurtured under the open sky in a life of work, enduring the sun, careless of shade, unacquainted with bathhouses, simple-souled, content with a little, with limbs toughened to endure every kind of toil, and for whom wielding iron, digging a ditch and carrying a burden is what they are used to from the country. (Vegetius, *Epitome*, 1.3, after Milner 1996)

Indeed, Tacitus asserts that the mutiny of the Rhine legions in AD 14 was exacerbated by the presence of 'city-bred recruits swept from the capital [Rome] by the recent levy, familiar with licence and chafing at hardship, [who] began to influence the simple minds of the rest' (Tacitus, *Annals*, 1.31).

Height
The ideal height of the legionary was 6 Roman feet (1.77m; 5ft 9in.) and men of at least 5 Roman feet and 10 inches (1.72m; 5ft 7in.) were preferred in the first cohort (Vegetius, *Epitome*, 1.5). However, the reality was different. Nero's legio I Italica was notable for two reasons: its composition of Italian recruits and the fact that all the men were at least

six Roman feet in height (Suetonius, *Nero*, 19). That this is worthy of note suggests that men of smaller stature were regularly accepted into the other legions. The skeletal remains of a soldier who died in Pompeii in AD 79 suggest he was about 1.7m (5ft 7in.) tall, but a soldier from the fort at Velsen in Holland was 1.9m tall (c.6ft 2in.). He may have been a local recruit from the Frisii. Evidence from the 4th century AD shows that men of 1.65m (5ft 5in.) were admitted into the elite units of the army, suggesting that this was actually the upper limit of height in the rural population from which recruits were drawn (*Theodosian Code*, 7.13.3).

Conscription

Many legionaries, if not the majority, were conscripts, and not necessarily educated to any great standard. The *dilectus* or levy was necessitated by the huge scale of the civil wars and the Augustan conquests (Brunt 1974). Volunteers were preferred but emperors were resigned to the necessity of conscription (Tacitus, *Annals*, 4.4).

A legionary recruit was supposed to be a Roman citizen but the civil wars had resulted in the wide dispersion of the legions and the need for rival commanders to recruit on the spot. For example, in 52 BC Julius Caesar raised legio V Alaudae from native Gauls; only later did he enfranchise them (Suetonius, *Caesar*, 24). The largest source of Roman citizens was Italy. From 40 BC this fundamental recruiting ground was denied to Mark Antony but his substantial force of legions, at least 23 at the time of Actium, had to be maintained and local sources were exploited – Syria, Galatia and Egypt. The real requirement for entry into the legions, whether as a conscript or volunteer, was free birth, not Roman citizenship; citizenship could be granted at enlistment or at some point during service. The Galatian legion XXII Deiotariana was not formed from Roman citizens. Its soldiers were subjects of, or mercenaries, serving the independent kingdom of Galatia until its absorption into the Empire in 25 BC. Roman citizenship would have been granted at the time of transfer.

In AD 23 the Emperor Tiberius bemoaned the lack of suitable Italian recruits coming forward to serve in the legions and announced his intention to tour the provinces in order to discharge the large number of eligible veterans, and to replenish the legions by conscription (Tacitus, *Annals*, 4.4). That so many soldiers were eligible for discharge suggests they had been recruited in large-scale levies more than 20 years before. Similarly, in AD 65 the urgent need to replenish manpower in the Illyrian legions after discharges attracted the attention of the Emperor Nero, suggesting that the veterans had been conscripted en

Dupondius of Gaius (Caligula), AD 37–41, celebrating the recapture of military standards lost to the Germans in AD 9 by his father Germanicus in AD 14–16. (Hunter Coin Cabinet, University of Glasgow)

masse 25 years before (service had been extended; *Annals*, 13.40). If long-established units were maintained by voluntary recruitment this should have meant a minimal number of annual discharges. In times of relative peace a legion of 5,000 men probably suffered a decremental mortality rate of about 40 per cent over a 25-year service period (indicative of the endemic diseases in the Roman world), and a further 15 per cent through soldiers invalided out of service. Consequently the legion would require 280 recruits annually to maintain optimum strength (Scheidel 1996: 117–24). This level of recruitment can hardly have troubled the emperors. They had problems because every 20 or 25 years they had to replenish much of a legion's strength at a single stroke.

Tiberius' complaint also reveals that Italy was no longer considered the major source of manpower for the Roman Army. While legions based in the west still drew substantially from Italy but increasingly from local sources, the legions in the east, particularly in Egypt, recruited from provincial sources from their beginnings. An important inscription of Augustan date from Egypt records the names and origins of 36 legionaries from III Cyrenaica and XXII Deiotariana (*ILS* 2483). The men specify origins in Asia Minor (20 soldiers), Egypt (7), Syria (2), Gallia Narbonensis (2), *castris* (2), Cyrenaica (1), Cyprus (1) and Italy (1). Only three of the legionaries originated in the west, and one from Italy itself (Vercellae); perhaps these three men were the only Roman citizens at enlistment. The majority of recruits came from Asia Minor, and were made citizens and given Roman names on enlistment. The two legions were also receiving local Egyptian recruits, but most notable are the two legionaries born *castris* – in the camp. These men were the sons of soldiers and their presence indicates to a certain extent that, despite the official ban on marriages, the sons of legionaries were readily accepted into service (Dio, 60.24; Tacitus *Annals*, 14.27).

TRAINING

We see no other explanation of the conquest of the world by the Roman People than their military training, camp discipline and practice in warfare.

(Vegetius, *Epitome*, 1.1)

Legionary recruits trained daily for four gruelling months. Training began with practising the military steps, 'for nothing should be maintained more on the march or in battle, than that all soldiers keep ranks as they move' (Vegetius, *Epitome*, 1.9). Recruits were required to march 29km in five hours at the regular step, and 35km in five hours at the faster step, loaded with a pack about 20.5kg (45lb) in weight. This burden was merely for acclimatisation; the weight of his arms and armour alone could be far greater. Strict maintenance of the ranks was enforced during drill, the centurions and training officers using their staffs to beat any laggards.

Once the recruits could march in time and follow the commands relayed by the trumpets and standards, manoeuvres were practised endlessly. They practised different formations: the hollow square, wedge, circle and the *testudo* ('the tortoise' – a mobile formation entirely protected by a roof and walls of shields). They were trained in overcoming obstacles, in charging and breaking off combat, in changing lines and relieving engaged units. The recruit was also taught to spring out of the line – this might prove useful in combat (Plutarch, *Antony*, 45).

Weapons training was conducted with swords, javelins and shields made of wood and wicker but twice the weight of the real thing. These weapons were used against 1.8m (6ft) practice posts. The instructors emphasised covering the body effectively with the shield while using the sword point instead of the edge, for this caused deeper wounds and was more efficient than slashing. Weapons training might occur twice a day.

If possible, recruits were also taught to swim so that a campaigning army's advance would not be impeded by rivers. They were also given cursory instruction in archery, the sling and riding, so that they had knowledge of all arms.

Drill was maintained when the recruit became a regular, and he was expected to complete three route marches every month. At the end of these marches soldiers constructed a fortified camp with ditches and earthen ramparts. This, with its orderly internal structure, was fundamental to Roman military practice (Vegetius, *Epitome*, 1.8–28, 2.5, 23–24).

The training that Roman soldiers underwent in advance of campaigns, and the daily weapons drill they performed when marching towards the war-zone, was crucial. This was especially true in peacetime because units were often under-strength, sometimes half their optimum size. Many soldiers were detached on various duties across the province, providing garrisons and acting as police (*stationarii*), or employed in various building projects, tax collecting or performing bureaucratic tasks for the provincial administration. Endemic disease also resulted in a steady rate of attrition. Only when a legion was required to fight in a major war might the majority of its manpower ever be assembled together, and its sub-units perform the manoeuvres they might carry out in battle (e.g. Josephus, *Jewish War*, 3.81ff).

LENGTH OF SERVICE

During the 1st century BC, until the battle of Actium in 31 BC, service in the legions normally lasted six years, but Augustus steadily increased this.

In 14 BC a huge area of land in Italy was requisitioned to settle legionary veterans, causing immense resentment, dislocation and poverty for the civilians involved (Dio, 54.25.4–5). The number of veterans was clearly substantial, and the date suggests that these men had enrolled in the new Imperial legions following the battle of Actium in 30 BC, completing 16 years of service. Augustus was following an earlier Republican precedent to retain soldiers for a longer period: 16 years was the normal upper limit of service in the legions in the 3rd and 2nd centuries BC (Polybius, 6.19.2). The situation was formalised in 13 BC: legionaries were to serve 16 years and receive a large cash bonus to avoid further discord over land settlement (Dio, 54.25.5–6). However, once a man had served 16 years he had to spend another four years in the legion's corps of veterans, the *vexillum veteranorum* (*ILS* 2649; Tacitus, *Annals*, 1.36).

By AD 5–6 Augustus increased service to 20 years, but the *praemia militiae* (discharge bonus) was increased to 12,000 sesterces (3,000 denarii) (Dio, 55.23.1). The extensive conquests in central Europe, and the need to consolidate them from 16 BC onwards, resulted in soldiers being retained far beyond the nominal term. It is clear that men continued to serve in excess of 20 years, and this was a major cause of the mutinies of AD 14:

> White haired men, many who have lost a limb from wounds, are in their thirtieth and fortieth year of service. Even after discharge their soldiering does not end, but remaining under the standards [i.e. *vexilla veteranorum*] they continue to endure the old hardships under a different name. (Tacitus, *Annals*, 1.17)

By the middle of the 1st century legionary service was fixed at 25 years, serving veterans being phased out. Some legionaries had to serve for 26 years because discharges were biennial and fell on 'even' years.

PAY

In AD 14 the basic legionary salary was 900 sesterces (225 denarii), paid in three instalments over the course of the year. The discharge bonus was around 12,000 sesterces (3,000 denarii). Under-officers and specialists within the legions received pay-and-a-half or double pay (*sesquiplicarii* and *duplicarii*). Deductions were made for the cost of equipment, clothing, food, burial fees, and a fixed sum went to the 'regimental savings bank' overseen by the *signiferi* (Vegetius, *Epitome*, 2.20). Pay was not increased until the reign of the Emperor Domitian (AD 81–96) and might never have been received fully by the soldiers even after deductions (Alston 1994). Discharge bonuses did not always materialise and soldiers might be fobbed off with plots of poor-quality land: 'under the name of "farm" some swampy morass or barren mountain side' (Tacitus, *Annals*, 1.17).

LEADERSHIP AND MORALE

The Roman legion is often described as a military machine, but the legion was only as good as the sum of its men and this was dependent on their morale. Legionaries were as apt to panic and as susceptible to defeat as any other demoralised soldiers throughout history. For example, when the army of Aulus Caecina was retreating through Germany in AD 15, it found itself in a situation similar to that which had destroyed the army of Varus. The Roman soldiers despaired:

> There were no tents for the centuries, no dressings for the wounded, and as they divided their rations, foul with dirt or blood, they bewailed the deathlike gloom and that for so many thousands of men but a single day remained. A stray horse that had taken fright at their shouting and broken free of its tether, threw into confusion the men who ran to stop it. So great was the

consequent panic – men believed the Germans had broken in – that there was a general rush to the gates ... principally the gate facing away from the enemy. (Tacitus, *Annals*, 1.65–66)

Commanders had to act quickly to stem the onset of panic and despair. The forbearance of Caecina held his army together:

Caecina, satisfied that their fear was groundless, still found command, entreaty and even force to no avail, threw himself flat in the gateway; and only shame barred a road that led over the general's body. At the same time the tribunes and centurions explained that it was a false alarm. He now paraded the soldiers in front of his headquarters, ordering them to listen in silence, warning them of the crisis and its urgency. 'Salvation lies in our arms, but we must be careful and remain within the rampart till the enemy approaches, hoping to storm the camp. Then we will erupt from all sides and make for the Rhine! If we flee, we can expect more forests, deeper swamps and a brutal enemy. But if victorious, glory and honour!' He reminded them of all they loved at home, all the honour they had gained in camp, but said nothing of their adversity. Then, with complete impartiality and beginning with his own, he distributed the horses of the legates and tribunes to men of great bravery. These were to charge first, followed by the infantry. (Tacitus, *Annals*, 1.66–67)

Caecina's plan succeeded. As the unsuspecting Germans debated how to assault the camp, the Romans charged down the ramparts, routing and pursuing their enemy until nightfall (Tacitus, *Annals*, 1.63–68).

Legionaries thrived on the charismatic and fair leadership of their officers. Caesar, Antony, Germanicus, Caecina and Vespasian are obvious examples of generals willing to lead by example and share the soldiers' hardships. The centurions frequently cited by Caesar and Josephus were courageous and steady, able to assert their authority in crisis situations and avert the onset of panic among the rank and file. But not all officers had the necessary confidence, courage or charisma to lead their men effectively. Many were brutal and corrupt. When fair leadership was lacking, performance in battle was poor and legionaries were readily disposed towards mutiny and rebellion.

Velleius Paterculus, who served as a legionary legate during the Illyrian Revolt of AD 6–9, emphasises that the disintegration and destruction of Quinctilius Varus' army in the Teutoburg Forest (AD 9) was caused by the poor leadership and cowardice of Varus and his senior officers:

An army unexcelled in bravery, the first of the Roman armies in discipline, energy and experience in the field, through negligence of its general, the treachery of the enemy and the unkindness of Fortune was surrounded, nor was as much opportunity as they had wished given to the soldiers either of fighting or of extricating themselves, except against heavy odds; indeed, some were even chastised for using their weapons and showing the spirit of the Romans. Hemmed in by forest, marshes and ambuscades, it was destroyed almost to a man by the very enemy it had always slaughtered like cattle. ... the general had more courage to die than to fight ... [and] ran himself through with his sword. The two camp prefects ... after most of the army had been destroyed, proposed its surrender, preferring to die by torture ... than in battle. [The legate] Vala Numonius ... previously an honourable man, set a fearful example by leaving the infantry unprotected by the cavalry, attempting to flee to the Rhine. Fortune avenged his act ... he died in the act of desertion. Varus' body, partially burned, was mutilated by the enemy; his head cut off. (Velleius Paterculus, 2.119)

The mutiny of the Pannonian legions at Emona in AD 14 was caused in part by the corruption and brutality of centurions and senior officers. The mutineer Percennius complained that from his pay he had to 'buy clothes, weapons and tents, [and] bribe the bullying centurion to purchase a respite from duty.' His comrades killed the centurion Lucilius, who was known as 'Fetch Another' because of his habit of breaking vine sticks while flogging legionaries and calling for a replacement (Tacitus, *Annals*, 1.17, 23). The excessive discipline of the camp prefect, Aufidienus Rufus, was repaid in kind. He was seized by a detachment of legionaries repairing roads and bridges:

Gravestone of Marcus Caelius of legio XVIII, killed in the Varian disaster in AD 9. Found near the legionary base at Xanten, Holland (ILS 2244). A centurion of the first cohort, Caelius wears a civic crown of oak leaves, a reward for saving a fellow-citizen in battle. (Landesmuseum, Bonn)

> Dragged from his carriage, loaded with baggage and driven at the head of the column, he was plied with sarcastic enquiries whether he found it pleasant to support these huge burdens and these endless marches. For Rufus, long an ordinary soldier, then centurion and ultimately camp prefect, sought to reintroduce the old hard discipline; he was habituated to work and toil and pitiless because he had endured. (Tacitus, *Annals*, 1.20)

The corruption of centurions also undermined the morale of Otho's legions in AD 69:

> The soldiers demanded that the payments usually made to centurions to secure leave should be abolished, since they amounted to an annual tax on ordinary soldiers. A quarter of each century would be away on leave or loafing about the camp itself, provided the soldiers paid the centurion his price, and

no-one cared how the burden pressed on the soldiers or how they got their money. In reality it was through highway robbery, petty thieving and by menial jobs that the soldiers purchased rest from military service. The richest soldiers would be assigned the worst fatigues until they purchased relief. Then impoverished and demoralised by idleness, the soldier returned to his century poor instead of wealthy and lazy instead of energetic. So ruined one after the other by the same poverty and lack of discipline, they were ready to rush into mutiny and dissension and ultimately into civil war. But Otho wished to avoid alienating the centurions, so he promised that the imperial treasury would pay for annual leave, a procedure which was undoubtedly useful and later established by good emperors as a fixed rule of service. (Tacitus, *Histories*, 1.46)

Even when corruption and brutality were (apparently) lacking, legionaries were unwilling to follow particular officers into battle. There is a strong impression that the flight of a cohort of legio III Augusta from an engagement against Tacfarinas in AD 18, was influenced not only by the number of the enemy, but by the unwillingness of the legionaries to follow a glory-seeking officer:

[Tacfarinas] invested a Roman cohort not far from the River Pagyda *(Tunisia)*. The fort was commanded by Decrius, who, energetic, vigorous and experienced in war, considered the siege a disgrace. After addressing the men, he drew up his lines in front of the fort and offered battle. As the cohort broke on the first onset, he darted eagerly among the missiles to intercept the fugitives, cursing the standard-bearers who could see Roman soldiers turn their backs to a horde of untrained men and deserters. At the same time, he turned … with one eye pierced, to confront the enemy and fought until he dropped, deserted by his men. (Tacitus, *Annals*, 3.20)

Legionaries did not want to follow men who could get them killed unnecessarily.

BELIEF AND BELONGING

Unit identity

Unit identity at the level of the legion was fostered by numerals and titles. It is notable that Augustus retained the numerals of the legions kept under arms after Actium. Previously, when legions were only in commission for about six years, numerals were recycled amongst the next levy. Also, not until the middle of the 1st century BC, when legions were in longer commission, did they acquire honorific titles to complement their numerals. One of the most famous legions of the civil wars of 49–42 BC was the legio Martia. Its honorific epithet, meaning 'war-like', became so defining that the actual numeral of the legion is unknown. The legion was lost at sea in 42 BC.

Legionaries came to be identified by the numerals or titles of their legion (see Tacitus, *Histories*, 2.43). Identity was enhanced by the veneration of specific emblems, perhaps alluding to founders (the Bull for Caesar's III Gallica, or the Capricorn for Augustus' XIV Gemina), or to their battle honours (the elephant of V Alaudae or the dolphin and warship of X Fretensis). The annual birthday feast celebrating the foundation of the legion (*natalis aquilae*, 'birthday of the eagle'), parades and training exercises were of fundamental importance in fostering mass unit identity and maintaining morale at the level of the legion, because these might be the only times outside of war when the full unit gathered together.

Group identity

What made the legionary truly effective in battle was his feeling of belonging to his century and in particular to his *contubernium*. Such identification with the unit and loyalty to the group of fellow soldiers was crucial to his performance in battle. The legionary fought first for his comrades, his century and legion, then for booty and glory, and lastly for the often distant emperor and the *Res Publica* (Roman state).

The close bonds between the eight men of the *contubernium* would have been strong simply by virtue of having to share a cramped single room together in barracks, or a tent on campaign. The other crucial bonding aspect of the *contubernium* was that it was a mess group. The Roman Army had no general messes for its soldiers, no dining halls in its fortresses or mass catering facilities when on campaign. Roman soldiers were expected to prepare their own meals and had to pay for food by deductions from their wages. As well as the pleasure of eating together, we can imagine the soldiers discussing (or complaining about) the day's duties: this was also essential to the fostering of group identity.

These bonds, created within the fort or camp, in training, daily duties, and at leisure and meal times in the close proximity of the barracks, initially bound men together as comrades. War and battle solidified them. The legionaries in the century fought effectively because they were well known to each other as friends and comrades – the century was not such a large unit that it became faceless and impersonal. Moreover the legionaries took pride in their collective centurial identity. They were their own elite within the legion and were driven by the bonds of comradeship not to let their fellow soldiers down in battle, to stand and fight for the men around them.

The terms for comradeship in the Roman Army are notable. *Contubernalis*, meaning tent- or mess-mate within the *contubernium* of eight legionaries, expressed not only the most basic group and social ties within the legion but also the dependency of *contubernales* upon each other in battle. *Commilito* (fellow-soldier) was perhaps the most binding term, for it was applied across the spectrum from the ordinary soldier (*miles*) to the general and, most importantly, the emperor. *Commilito* spoke of the unity of the army and of respect for fellow soldiers whatever their rank. However, a most interesting occurrence of *commilito* is found on the funerary urn of an Augustan soldier. The brevity of this text emphasises the unjust death of a soldier by another in the same army and the betrayal of comradeship:

L. Hepenius L. f. ocisus ab comilitone *[sic]*.
'Lucius Hepenius, son of Lucius, killed by a fellow soldier.'

The urn was discovered in a tomb at Asciano, south-east of Siena, and contained a coin dating to 15 BC, suggesting death during the reign of Augustus. It has been supposed that Hepenius was a praetorian or a soldier of the Urban Cohorts who was killed in Rome and whose ashes were returned to his family for burial (Keppie 2000: 317).

Manipularis or *commanipularis* (soldier in the same maniple) implied the reliance of legionaries upon each other, and century upon century, for success and survival in battle. The most poignant term, regularly inscribed on tombstones, was *frater* (brother). On many such monuments it is clear from the different family names of the deceased and the heir(s) that they could not have been actual brothers, but the term expresses with great eloquence and simplicity the fundamental bonds between comrades. If the legion can be described as a society, the *contubernium* was the family of the legionary.

Fraternity between comrades could extend to the extremes of mass suicide. In AD 28 400 auxiliaries trapped in a villa complex by the Frisii chose to fall on each other's swords rather than be taken by the enemy (Tacitus, *Annals*, 4.73). In 54 BC one of Caesar's legions and five other legionary cohorts were destroyed when trying to evacuate the territory of the Eburones. Some legionaries managed to fight their way back to their abandoned winter camp and to repel the assaults of the Gauls until nightfall, but rather than be overrun they chose to commit suicide (Caesar, *Gallic War*, 5.37). Appian gives an insight into the soldiers' view of suicide. He relates that soldiers of the renowned legio Martia committed suicide in defiance of what they saw as a useless death when their transport ships were fired and sunk by the fleet of Sextus Pompeius in 42 BC:

Some of the soldiers, especially the Martians, who excelled in bravery, were exasperated that they should lose their lives uselessly, and so killed themselves [rather] than be burned to death. Others leaped on board the vessels of the enemy, selling their lives dearly. (Appian, *Civil Wars*, 4.116)

This choice of suicide appears to have been quite honourable, a way of cheating the enemy of total victory and could even be viewed as a means of maintaining the honour of the army. During the siege of Jerusalem the Jews trapped a large number of Roman soldiers by setting fire to the portico in which they were fighting, cutting off their line of retreat. Most burned to death or were cut down by the Jews but Longus escaped:

The Jews, in their admiration of Longus' prowess and from their inability to kill him, besought him to come down ... pledging him his life. His brother Cornelius ... implored him not to disgrace his own reputation or Roman arms. Influenced by his words, he brandished his sword in view of both armies and slew himself. (Josephus, *Jewish War*, 6.185–88)

Above all, such episodes illustrate how the ties that bound a unit together remained even in times of greatest stress and terror, that a man would rather die in a pact with his fellow soldiers than be taken by the enemy. Even suicide stimulated by shame, for example that of the apparently cowardly soldier recalled by Suetonius (*Otho*, 10), could be viewed as redemptive and as the ultimate expression of comradeship. Suetonius Laetus, father of the biographer Suetonius, served as tribune of legio XIII Gemina during the civil war of AD 69. He recalled an episode when a messenger reported to the Emperor Otho the defeat of his forces near Cremona:

Aureus issued by Vespasian, AD 70, showing *signiferi* of different units shaking hands in the aftermath of the civil wars of AD 68–70, with the legend 'the army in agreement'. (Hunter Coin Cabinet, University of Glasgow)

> When the garrison [at Brixellum] called him a liar and a cowardly deserter, the man fell on his sword at Otho's feet. At this sight, Otho, my father reported, cried out that he would never again risk the lives of such courageous men, who had deserved so well. (Suetonius, *Otho*, 10)

Otho himself went on to commit suicide.

In times of war the concept of fraternity was extended and soldiers fought in support of other units as well as their immediate comrades. A notable example occurred in AD 28 when during a disastrous battle fought mainly by auxiliary units against the Frisii, legio V mounted a counter-attack and extricated a large number of the auxiliaries. However, 900 auxiliaries could not escape and fought to the end (Tacitus, *Annals*, 4.73; not to be confused with the 400 who committed suicide). Velleius Paterculus' epitaph for the legions XVII, XVIII and XIX lost in AD 9, indicates their cohesion as a battle group: 'they were the bravest of all the armies.' (2.119.2)

SACRAMENTUM, DECORATIONS AND PUNISHMENTS

The military oath

Here we should recall the oath sworn by all Roman soldiers, the *sacramentum*. The oath had religious significance and bound the soldier to the emperor and the state. It was repeated annually on New Year's Day. Vegetius summarises the Christianised version of the 4th century AD:

> They swear by God, Christ and the Holy Spirit, and by the Majesty of the Emperor which second to God is to be loved and

worshipped by the human race. ... The soldiers swear that they will strenuously do all that the Emperor may command, will never desert the service, nor refuse to die for the Roman State (Vegetius, *Epitome*, 2.5, after Milner 1996).

Until the institution of a formal and legally binding oath in 216 BC, legionaries had sworn two voluntary oaths. The first was to obey the consul; the second they swore to one another within the maniple: never to desert comrades in order to save yourself, never to abandon your place in the battle line unless to recover a weapon, attack an enemy or to save a comrade (Livy, 22.38). Despite later forms of the oath directing the loyalty of legionaries to the commander and state, the sentiments of the earlier oath were adhered to in the centuries of the late Republic and early Empire. Caesar emphasises that the centurions Pullo and Vorenus, bitter rivals for rank and honours, 'despite their enmity each helped to save the other [in battle]' (Caesar, *Gallic War*, 5.44).

Rewards and decorations

The highest decoration available to the legionary, irrespective of rank, was the *corona civica* – the civic crown of oak leaves awarded for saving the life of a fellow-citizen in battle. No act of bravery in battle was viewed as so important or so selfless as forcing back the enemy to save a fallen comrade. It was the epitome of comradeship, illustrating for whom the legionaries really fought: each other. This was the essence of the effectiveness of the army. Marcus Helvius Rufus was famously awarded the *corona civica* by the Emperor Tiberius for saving the life of a fellow veteran legionary in a battle against Tacfarinas in AD 20:

> When ... the forces of Tacfarinas assaulted a stronghold named Thala, they were routed by a detachment of [legionary] veterans [*vexillum veteranorum*] not more than 500 in number. During the battle a common soldier, Helvius Rufus, earned the distinction of saving a fellow citizen, and was presented by [*governor*] Apronius with a *torque* and spear. The civic crown was added by the emperor [Tiberius], who regretted, more in sorrow than anger, that [Apronius] had not exercised his power to award this further honour. (Tacitus, *Annals*, 3.21)

Rufus is the last ordinary legionary known to have received such a spear, as the reward was soon confined to officers. An inscription from his hometown of Varia in Italy reveals that Rufus was later promoted to *primus pilus* and that he had added *Civica* to his name (*ILS* 2637). Such acts of pride were not uncommon. Legionaries who had fought for Octavian at Actium added the appellation Actiacus, 'Actium-fighter', to their names:

> Marcus Billienus Actiacus, son of Marcus, of the voting tribe Romula, served in legio XI, fought in the naval battle [Actium], was settled in the colony [Este, Italy, 30 BC], selected as town councillor. (*ILS* 2243)

Polybius notes that the Romans encouraged valour by the awarding of decorations, and ensured that soldiers were conspicuous to their

commanders on the battlefield by the wearing of animal skins (*velites*/skirmishers), or crests and feathers (regular legionaries) (Polybius, 6.22–23, 39). Decorations for valour available to all ranks included *torques* (neck-bands or collars) and *phalerae* (medals) worn on a harness, and *armillae* (bracelets/armbands) of precious metal, as well as grants of money and promotions. The awarding of other crowns, spears and flags were increasingly restricted to centurions and higher officers (Maxfield 1981). Titus distributed such rewards in a ceremony following the capture and destruction of Jerusalem in AD 70:

> [He] gave orders to the appointed officers to read out the names of all who had performed any courageous act during the war. Calling forward each by name he applauded them as they came forward, no less exultant over their exploits than if they were his own. He then placed gold crowns on their heads, presented them with golden torques, little golden spears and standards made of silver, and promoted each man to a higher rank. He further assigned to them out of the spoils of silver and gold and fine clothing and other booty in abundance. (Josephus, *Jewish War*, 7.13–16)

On parade and in battle Roman soldiers wore their decorations with pride. Decorations feature prominently in Tacitus' description of the entry of Vitellius' victorious army into Rome in July AD 69:

The eagles of four legions were at the head of the column, while the flags *(vexilla)* of the detachments of four other legions were on either side. … Before the eagles marched the camp prefects, tribunes and chief centurions dressed in white. The other centurions, with polished arms and decorations gleaming, marched with their centuries. The ordinary soldiers' *phalerae* and torques were likewise bright and shining. It was an imposing sight and an army that deserved a better emperor than Vitellius. (Tacitus, *Histories*, 2.89)

Such decorations were prized items of plunder. One of Caesar's continuators describes how the decorations of a brave centurion were taken during the fighting against the Pompeians before Munda (45 BC):

When it was observed that our men were giving more ground than was usual, two centurions from legio V crossed the river [Salsum] and restored the battle line. As they drove the superior numbers of enemy back displaying exceptional courage … one of them succumbed to a heavy volley of missiles discharged from higher ground. His fellow centurion now began an unequal battle, and when he found himself completely surrounded he retreated but lost his footing. As the brave centurion fell many of the enemy rushed forward to strip him of his decorations ('Caesar', *Spanish War*, 23).

Punishments

Discipline was enforced with severity. Cowardice in battle and other derelictions of duty, such as falling asleep on guard duty, were punished by *fustuarium* (being beaten to death by comrades whose lives had been endangered), floggings and demotions (see Polybius, 6.35–38). If a complete unit displayed cowardice in battle it might suffer decimation, when every tenth man was selected by lot and executed. This was a rare and extreme punishment but occurred as late as AD 18 (Tacitus, *Annals*, 3.21). Other punishments were more symbolic, intended to shame offenders, such as putting soldiers on rations of detested barley or ostracising them from military life by making them camp outside the ramparts (Plutarch, *Antony*, 39; Frontinus, *Stratagems*, 4.1). They might be stripped of their military belts (i.e. their military identity) and forced to parade outside the headquarters wearing heavy helmets and holding out long, heavy staffs or sods of turf (Suetonius, *Augustus*, 24). Only when soldiers had redeemed themselves in battle might these punishments be revoked.

Bravado and initiative

In a perverse way, despite the emphasis placed on discipline and maintaining the cohesion of the battle line, the Roman Army tolerated, and in some ways encouraged, acts of dangerous bravado and allowed its soldiers a surprising degree of personal initiative. When Quintus Cicero's legion was besieged by the Nervii in 54 BC, Caesar indicates that the bravery of the centurions Pullo and Vorenus was an inspiration to all:

There were two courageous centurions ... Titus Pullo and Lucius Vorenus. They quarrelled continually about who came first [in rank] and every year fiercely contested the most important posts. ... When the fighting by the ramparts was intense, Pullo said, 'Why hesitate, Vorenus? What chance of proving your bravery are you waiting for? This day will decide our contest.' So speaking, he left the defences and charged where the Gauls were thickest. Neither did Vorenus remain within the rampart, following Pullo for fear of what men would think. Then, at close range, Pullo threw his *pilum* at the enemy, skewering one Gaul who had run forward from the multitude. [But Pullo was soon] knocked senseless and the enemy sought to cover him with their shields and they all threw their missiles at him, giving him no chance of retreat. Pullo's shield was pierced and a javelin was lodged in his belt. Vorenus, his rival, ran to him and helped him out of trouble. Vorenus fought with his *gladius* at close-quarters, killing one and drove the others back a little. But he pressed on too eagerly and fell into a hollow. He was surrounded in turn, but Pullo came to his aid. They killed several men and retired to the ramparts with the utmost glory. In the eagerness of their rivalry Fortune so handled them that, despite their hostility, each helped and saved the other, and it was impossible to decide which should be considered the braver man. (Caesar, *Gallic War*, 5.44)

Soldiers probably acted without or contrary to orders simply because of the lack of communication on the battlefield. Yet it is clear that independent actions could have important effects on the outcome of engagements. During the siege of Gamala in AD 67, three soldiers of legio XV Apollinaris, acting without orders, managed one night to prise five key supporting stones from the base of a corner tower causing it to collapse and securing the Roman capture of the city (Josephus, *Jewish War*, 4.63–66). At the second battle of Cremona two Flavian legionaries took up the shields of casualties of the Vitellian legion XV Primigenia, and thus disguised they advanced on the Vitellian line and disabled a massive *ballista* (torsion catapult) which had stopped the Flavians' advance. The soldiers were killed in this act (Tacitus, *Histories*, 3.23). Such acts served to bolster morale and unit pride, and the general Suetonius Paulinus noted that the outcome of battles might indeed hinge on the deeds of a few legionaries (Tacitus, *Annals*, 14.36).

DRESS AND APPEARANCE

The military identity of individual soldiers was conferred not by a uniform – the soldier's clothing of tunic and cloak was little different to that of the civilian – but by the military belt (*balteus*) and boots (*caligae*).

The *balteus* took the form of either a single waist belt decorated with silvered, sometimes embossed, bronze plates, or two crossed belts slung from the hips. The date of the introduction of the cross belts is not certain; they may have appeared during the close of the reign of

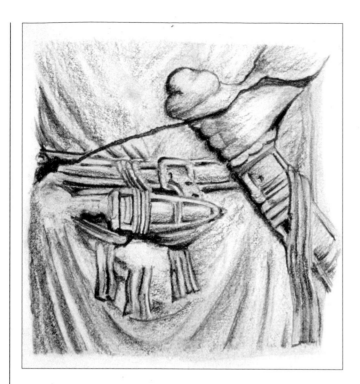

Detail of Lorarius' belt-fittings. The suspension of the dagger over the abdomen is unique. The arrangement of the belt ends anticipates the 'apron'. (Museo Civico, Padova. Drawn by Steven D. P. Richardson after Franzoni 1987, tav. XIV.1)

Augustus, to which the apron of studded straps belongs (the decorative plates for such an apron have been found at Kalkriese, site of the Varian disaster). It was probably during the reign of Tiberius that niello, a black alloy of sulphur and silver, lead or copper, began to be widely used to decorate belt plates with intricate inlaid designs (Deschler-Erb 2000). Such belts identified a man as a soldier; Juvenal characterised soldiers as 'armed and belted men' (*Satires*, 16.48). The removal of the *balteus* stripped a soldier of his military identity; it was confiscated if a soldier was dishonourably discharged (Herodian, 2.13.10). In Rome in AD 69 civilian pranksters used razor-sharp knives to slice through the belts of unassuming soldiers in a crowd. The soldiers went on the rampage when they realised what had happened and numerous civilians were killed, including the father of one legionary (Tacitus, *Histories*, 2.88).

Military boots, *caligae*, were the other key item of identification. The date of their introduction is uncertain, but they were certainly the standard footwear for the Roman soldier from the reign of Augustus until the early 2nd century AD. Really a heavy-duty sandal, the crunch of the iron-nailed sole identified the presence of a soldier as much as his jingling belts (Josephus, *Jewish War*, 6.85). Archaeological finds from across the Empire indicate that there was a major degree of standardisation in the form of *caligae* and the nailing pattern of soles, suggesting that pattern books for this, and perhaps other items of military equipment, were issued by the emperors. The nailing patterns, giving support to the ball, arch and heel of the foot, are viewed as the precursors of the sole patterns on modern training shoes.

Bronze belt buckles, Kalkriese, AD 9. (Varusschlacht im Osnabrücker Land, Museum und Park Kalkriese)

The colour of military tunics is much disputed. Evidence for centurions parading in white could refer to the wearing of fine linen tunics, or perhaps to the colour of crests and *pteruges* (fabric-strip defences for the upper arms, abdomen and thighs) (Tacitus, *Histories*, 2.89). Otherwise, the suggestion that centurions normally wore woollen tunics dyed red, and lower ranks wore off-white tunics is plausible (Fuentes 1987; *contra* Sumner 2002).

EQUIPMENT

The legionary is thought of primarily as a swordsman, charging forward into the enemy and using his sword to thrust rather than slash (Polybius, 2.33, 3.114; Vegetius, *Epitome*, 1.12). However, only the soldiers in the front rank would have been able to use their swords in battle, and battles were often characterised by lengthy missile duels.

Pilum

The *pilum* is the defining weapon of the Roman legionary. Unlike the *gladius*, which was a number of distinct and successive sword types, the *pilum* retained its two basic forms – tanged and socketed – for six centuries. A heavy javelin, *c.*2m (over 6ft) in length, it had a long iron shank (*c.*40–90cm) tipped with a pyramidal or barbed head. The *pilum* was a short-range weapon designed to punch through shields, armour and into the man beyond. It was essential to the Roman sword-fighting technique because the devastation caused by a volley of *pila* created the perfect conditions for the legionary to charge forward with his cut-and-thrust sword. Shorter, light *pila*, some with shanks only 15cm long, were probably used by legionary skirmishers.

A number of flat-tanged *pila* from the Augustan fort of Oberaden in Germany survive with much of their wooden shafts intact, and would

ABOVE **Silver-plated apron fittings and terminal, Kalkriese, AD 9. (Varusschlacht im Osnabrücker Land, Museum und Park Kalkriese)**

BELOW ***Pilum* head from Kalkriese, AD 9. (Varusschlacht im Osnabrücker Land, Museum und Park Kalkriese)**

RIGHT *Pilum* collets, Kalkriese, AD 9. (Varusschlact im Osnabrücker Land, Museum und Park Kalkriese)

BELOW **Roman missiles from Kalkriese, AD 9. From left, light javelin, two spear heads, three catapult bolt heads, *pilum* collet and butt-spike. (Varusschlacht im Osnabrücker Land, Museum und Park Kalkriese)**

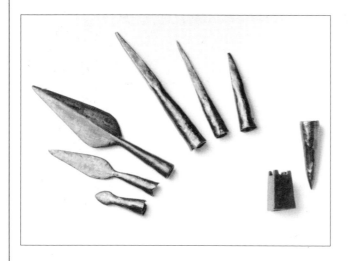

RIGHT **Mainz *principia* relief: light-armed legionary. (Landesmuseum, Mainz)**

have weighed about 2kg (4.4lb). However, examples from the late Republic, e.g. from Valencia, had much more substantial shanks and would have been considerably heavier. Some *pila* were fitted with a bulbous weight, probably of lead, but no archaeological examples have been identified. Such heavy *pila* are held by praetorians on a panel surviving from the lost Arch of Claudius in Rome, erected in celebration of the conquest of southern Britain. The heavy *pila* weighed at least 50 per cent more and resulted in a loss of range (maximum 30m, but better penetration at shorter distances). Clearly this was acceptable if penetration was increased.

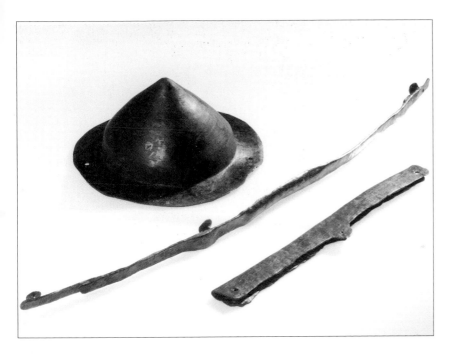

Shield

The traditional shield of the legionary was the curved, oval *scutum*. A 1st-century BC example from Fayum in Egypt measured 128cm long by 63.5cm wide and was made of strips of planed wood laminated in three alternate layers. The shield was slightly thicker in the centre (1.2cm; 1cm at the edges), and had a wooden 'spindel' boss. It was faced with felt and calf skin and weighed 10kg (22lb). During the Augustan period the shield was modified, eventually becoming a curved rectangular board. The only surviving example of this cylindrical type comes from Dura Europos in Syria, AD 255/7. It was constructed in exactly the same manner as the Fayum shield, measuring 102cm long by 83cm wide (66cm across the curve), but was a far lighter piece, only 5mm thick and weighing about 5.5kg (12.1lb). Peter

Connolly has suggested that earlier examples were thicker in the middle and weighed 7.5kg (16.5lb) (Connolly 1981: 233).

The weight of the *scutum* meant that it was held by the horizontal grip with a straight arm. It was primarily used offensively, legionaries barging into opponents and using the prominent boss to unbalance or topple them (Tacitus, *Annals*, 14.36; *Histories*, 2.42). At Mons Graupius the Batavian and Tungrian cohorts appear to have used their *umbones* (bosses) to punch at the Caledonians (Tacitus, *Agricola*, 36). The flat shields of the auxiliaries were not necessarily lighter than legionary models; the rectangular shield with a curved top from Hod Hill weighed about 9kg (19.8lb).

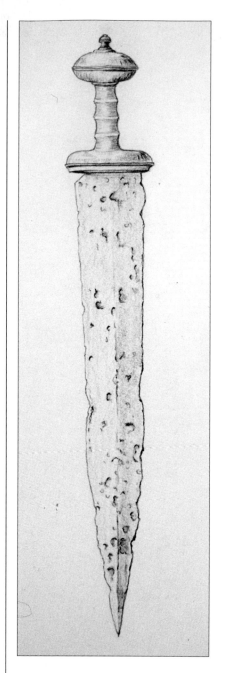

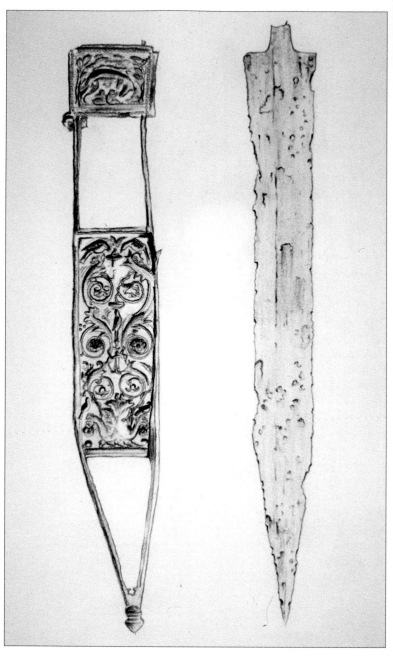

ABOVE LEFT **Mainz-type**
gladius **from Rheingönheim**
with silver-plated hilt. (Speyer,
Historisches Museum der Pfalz.
Drawn by Steven D. P. Richardson
after Ulbert 1969, abb. 3.1)

ABOVE RIGHT **Mainz-type**
gladius **with Romulus and Remus**
scabbard found in the Thames at
Fulham. (British Museum. Drawn
by Steven D. P. Richardson after
Ulbert 1969, taf. 32)

Sword

The Roman legionary is popularly assumed to have been armed with a
short stabbing sword know as the *gladius*, but this is a misconception. For
the Romans the word *gladius* simply meant 'sword', not specifically a
short sword. Indeed, Tacitus used *gladius* to refer to the long slashing
swords wielded by the Caledonians at Mons Graupius (*Agricola*, 36). The
famous Spanish sword, the *gladius Hispaniensis*, often referred to by
Polybius and Livy, was in fact a medium-length cut-and-thrust weapon,
with blade lengths of between 64cm and 69cm and widths of 4–5.5cm
(Connolly 1997: 49–56). The blade could have parallel edges or be
slightly waisted, the final fifth or so of its length tapering to a sharp

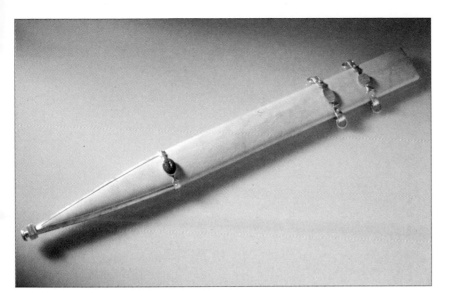

Restored scabbard fittings from Kalkriese, AD 9. (Varusschlacht im Osnabrücker Land, Museum und Park Kalkriese)

point. The longer swords must have weighed more than 1.5kg. This weapon, probably adopted by the Romans shortly after the battle of Cannae in 216 BC, was actually adapted by the Iberians from the Celtic long sword. The scabbard had a frame of sheet iron or bronze with wood or leather inserts, though bronze sheet is also known. Some Roman troops continued to employ the Spanish sword until about 20 BC (a notable example comes from Berry-Bouy in France), but it was quickly superseded in Augustus' reign by the Mainz/Fulham-type *gladius* (named after prominent find-spots). This sword was a clear development of the *gladius Hispaniensis*, but had a shorter and broader, waisted blade (c.40–56cm long, up to 8cm across the shoulders) with a notably long tapering point. Examples weigh between 1.2kg and 1.6kg. The metal scabbards of these swords could be tinned or silvered and finely embossed with various motifs, often derived from Augustan propaganda.

The short Pompeii-type *gladius* was introduced at the close of our period. It was a sword quite different from the Spanish and Mainz/Fulham *gladii* with its parallel edged blade and short triangular point (*c.*42–55cm long, 5–6cm wide), but legionaries clearly maintained the same cut-and-thrust fighting technique. This sword weighed about 1kg. The fine embossed scabbard of the Mainz/Fulham *gladius* gave way

Short-pointed *gladius* from Pompeii, AD 79. (Museo Nazionale di Napoli. Drawn by Steven D. P. Richardson after Ulbert 1969, taf. 17.1)

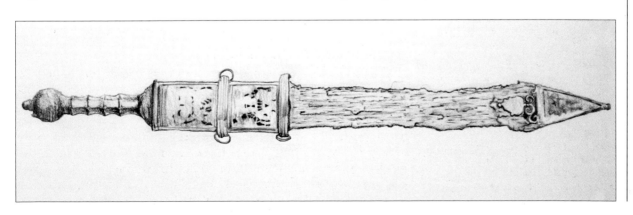

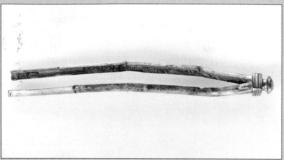

TOP LEFT **Scabbard clasp, Kalkriese, AD 9.** (Varusschlacht im Osnabrücker Land, Museum und Park Kalkriese)

TOP RIGHT **Scabbard clasp with intaglio from Kalkriese, AD 9.** (Varusschlacht im Osnabrücker Land, Museum und Park Kalkriese)

BOTTOM LEFT **Scabbard frame from Kalkriese, AD 9.** (Varusschlacht im Osnabrücker Land, Museum und Park Kalkriese)

BOTTOM RIGHT **Silver scabbard clasp from Kalkriese, with setting for a lost stone, AD 9.** (Varusschlacht im Osnabrücker Land, Museum und Park Kalkriese)

to a wood and leather construction with metal binding and chape, to which punched, engraved or embossed decoration was applied. All Roman swords in our period were attached to the belt or baldric via a four-ring suspension system. Being the predominant weapon on Trajan's Column, the Pompeii *gladius* has stuck in the imagination of many as the defining weapon of the legionary. Yet in terms of longevity it was perhaps the shortest lived of Roman swords; introduced in the mid-1st century, probably as a standardised pattern, it was already going out of use by the second quarter of the 2nd century.

Ordinary Roman soldiers wore their swords on the right; *aquiliferi*, centurions and more senior officers wore it on the left as a mark of their rank.

Dagger

Another adoption from the Spanish was the dagger (*pugio*). Like a miniature *gladius* with a waisted blade at least 20cm and up to 35cm in length, it was worn on the left hip (by ordinary legionaries), and its iron-frame scabbard employed the same method of ring suspension. From the Augustan period, dagger hilts and scabbards (now completely of metal) were decorated with increasingly fine silver and niello inlays. The basic form of this dagger was still in use in the 3rd century AD.

Armour

The majority of legionaries in the Imperial period fought in heavy body armour, though some troops did without armour at all. Caesar made use of such legionaries to fight as *antesignani*, that is lightly equipped legionaries (*expediti*) who skirmished with light missiles in front of the standards of the main battle line or reinforced the cavalry (e.g. at Pharsalus, *Civil War*, 3.75, 84). A relief from the legionary headquarters building (*principia*) at Mainz shows two legionaries fighting in close order, equipped with *scuta* and *pila*, but apparently without body armour, suggesting that even the 'heavy' legionaries could fight *expediti*.

Two other reliefs from Mainz reveal the regular armours employed by legionaries. In one scene a *legionarius* marching behind a *signifer* wears a cuirass of *lorica segmentata* (the term is modern), an articulated armour of iron plates and hoops. This is the armour worn exclusively by citizen troops on Trajan's Column but its use was never as total as that monument would suggest. Recent discoveries from Kalkriese, the site of the Varian disaster (near Osnabrück in Germany), including a complete chest plate edged with bronze, have shown that this armour was

ABOVE LEFT **Mainz *principia* relief: front-rank legionaries fighting *expediti*. (Landesmuseum, Mainz)**

ABOVE RIGHT **Gravestone of Flavoleius Cordus, legio XIV Gemina, equipped with oval shield and light javelin with a throwing-thong. Pre-AD 43. (Landesmuseum, Mainz)**

ABOVE LEFT **Mainz *principia* relief: legionary and *signifer* on the march. Mid-later 1st century AD. (Landesmuseum, Mainz)**

ABOVE RIGHT **Iron chest plate edged with bronze from a cuirass of *lorica segmentata*, Kalkriese, AD 9. (Varusschlacht im Osnabrücker Land, Museum und Park Kalkriese)**

developed under Augustus. Other fragments are now known from the Augustan bases at Haltern and Dangstetten in Germany. The cuirass offered substantial protection, especially to the shoulders and upper back, but necessarily terminated at the hips, leaving the abdomen and upper legs exposed. It is probable that some kind of padded garment was worn underneath to absorb the impact of blows, protect the skin from chafing and ensure that the armour was properly settled, so that the chest and other plates lined up correctly. Reconstructions of this armour suggest it weighed about 9kg (20lb).

Another relief from Mainz portrays a centurion (his sword is worn on the left) in what at first sight appears to be a tunic. However, the splits at the arms and thighs indicate that this was a ring mail shirt (*lorica hamata*), the splits necessary to facilitate movement. On many such monuments the actual details of the rings were originally painted in. Mail was probably the armour most widely used by the Romans. In our period shirts were sleeveless or short-sleeved and could extend far down the thighs, though lengths varied. Most legionaries wore shirts with a doubling over the shoulders of leather faced with mail, modelled after the shoulder guards of the Greek linen cuirass. Such shirts weighed 9–15kg (19.8–33lb), depending on the length and the number of rings (at least 30,000). Other shirts had full shoulder capes and might weigh 16kg (35.2lb). The weight placed on the shoulders was clearly substantial, but some of this could be transferred to the hips by the use of belts. Mail was normally made out of iron but bronze rings are also known, often used for decorative trims. Occasionally shirts were faced with fine scales. Scale was another common armour (*lorica squamata*), being cheaper and easier to produce than mail but inferior in defensive qualities and flexibility.

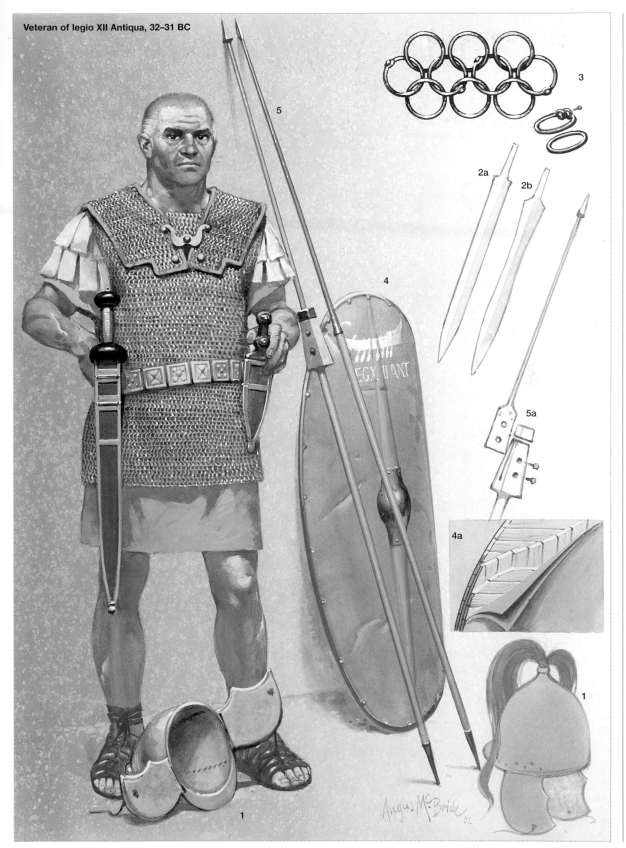

Veteran of legio XII Antiqua, 32–31 BC

A

Legionary press-gang in Ostia, port of Rome, AD 6–9

Contubernium on the march, post-AD 14

1

C

Legionary fighting techniques

Marching camp, 1st century AD

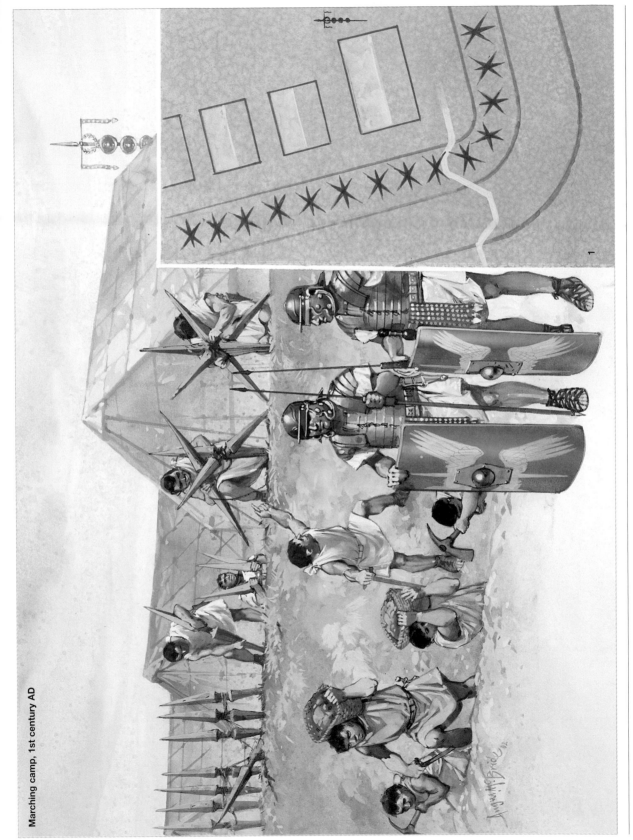

E

F

Battle of the Teutoburg Forest, Germany, autumn AD 9

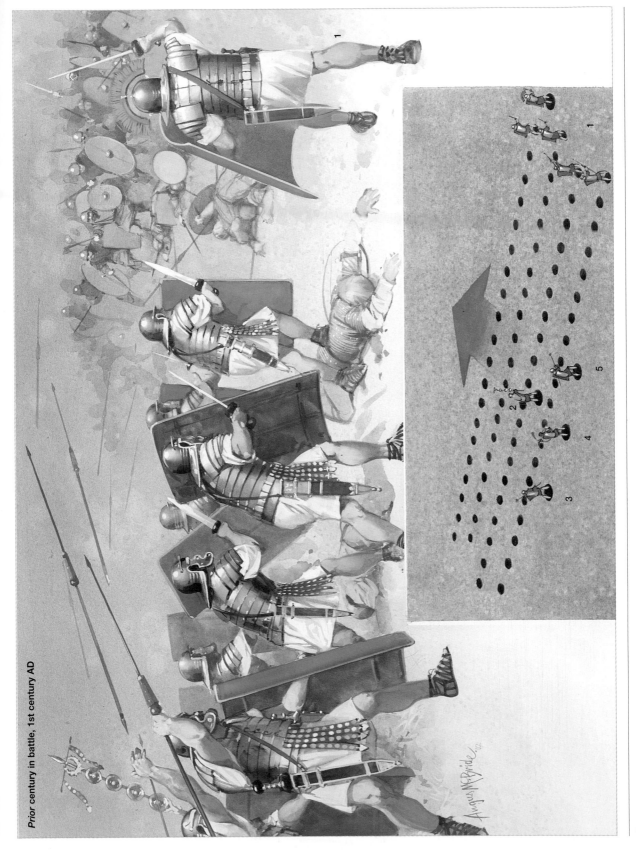

Prior century in battle, 1st century AD

G

Legionary of II Augusta,
Britain AD 43

4
4
5
7
2
9
3
6
8
1

Angus McBride '02

H

Such shirts were worn over an arming doublet known as a *subarmilis*, probably made of linen stuffed with wool. This helped absorb the shock of blows and prevented the metal of the armour being driven into the body (*De Rebus Bellicis*, 15). *Pteruges*, overlapping linen or leather strip defences for the upper legs and arms, were often attached to such garments, but could not prevent serious injuries to the limbs to which Roman soldiers were particularly susceptible (e.g. Caesar, *Gallic War*, 5.35). Greaves were regularly worn by centurions but not by lower ranks until the end of the 1st century AD and perhaps only against particular opponents such as the Dacians. Articulated arm defences (*manicae*) were certainly employed by gladiators in our period (Tacitus, *Annals*, 3.43–46, for the *cruppellarii* fighting for Sacrovir in AD 21), but might not have come into widespread military use until the reign of Domitian (AD 81–96).

Helmet

Legionaries wore a number of different types of helmet. At the beginning of our period bronze, occasionally iron, Montefortino helmets were common, the traditional legionary helmet since the 4th century BC. These had a single bowl with a very slight rear peak, and cheek pieces that covered the ears and protected the sides of the face. Later versions of the helmet, including the Coolus-type, were in use until the later 1st century AD, and had substantial neck guards and cheek pieces with flanges to protect the throat and cut-aways to facilitate hearing.

Early in the Augustan period, perhaps even during Caesar's conquest of Gaul, Roman smiths began to adapt Gallic Port and Agen-type iron

ABOVE LEFT **Mainz *principia* relief: a legionary, perhaps a centurion, wearing mail armour. (Landesmuseum, Mainz)**

ABOVE RIGHT (TOP) **Decorated iron mail hooks lost in the Varian disaster, AD 9. (Varusschlacht im Osnabrücker Land, Museum und Park Kalkriese)**

ABOVE RIGHT (BOTTOM) **Inscribed mail hooks, Kalkriese, AD 9. (Varusschlacht im Osnabrücker Land, Museum und Park Kalkriese)**

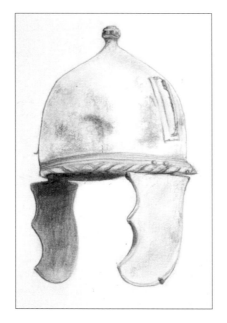

ABOVE LEFT **Imperial Gallic A helmet. (Rijksmuseum, Nijmegen. Drawn by Steven D. P. Richardson after Robinson 1975, pl. 102)**

ABOVE RIGHT **Imperial Italic C helmet from Cremona. (Museo Stibbert, Florence. Drawn by Steven D. P. Richardson after Robinson 1975, pl. 158)**

RIGHT **Montefortino-type helmet in the Museo Antichita, Parma, 4th–3rd century BC. An early example of a helmet widely used by Augustan legionaries. Drawn by Steven D. P. Richardson after Robinson 1975, pl. 4.**

FAR RIGHT **Iron Imperial Gallic A helmet discovered near the Augustan fort at Nijmegen in Holland, end 1st century BC. (Rijksmuseum, Nijmegen. Drawn by Steven D. P. Richardson after Robinson 1975, pl. 101)**

helmets for legionary use. These Imperial Gallic-type helmets were high-quality, single bowled pieces, with embossed 'eyebrows' at the front of the bowl and ridges at the nape of the neck to break the force of downward sword blows. The Romans added a substantial neck guard (really a rear peak), a brow peak, increased the size and curvature of the cheek pieces and also added throat flanges. Towards the middle of the 1st century AD a variant of this helmet was produced in Italian workshops, using both iron and bronze (a progression from the Italic Montefortino-type), and known as the Imperial Italic type (Robinson 1975: 13–81).

Legionary helmets were substantial pieces with bowls 1.5–2mm thick, weighing about 2–2.3kg (4.4–5.1lb). Helmets and cheek pieces were lined with woollen felt, and the fitting of some helmets may have allowed an air space between the skull and the bowl to dissipate the shock of blows. Montefortino-type helmets had broad cheek pieces that covered the ears, but the new Imperial Gallic helmets were soon made

to incorporate ear holes. However, unless a soldier had a helmet specially made or adapted, the cheek pieces might still partially cover his ears. While cheek pieces gave good protection to the sides of the face they could obscure peripheral vision, and the exposed centre of the face made a tempting target for opponents. The Batavian and Tungrian auxiliaries fighting at Mons Graupius stabbed at the faces of their British opponents (Tacitus, *Agricola*, 36) and Caesar records how the centurion Crastinus was killed at Pharsalus by a sword thrust to the mouth (Caesar, *Civil War*, 3.99).

The burden of equipment

The mental strain of battle cannot have been helped by the immense total weight of the fighting equipment borne by an Augustan legionary (see table).

Wearing *lorica segmentata* and carrying a curved rectangular *scutum* could reduce the burden to about 23kg (50.6lb). On the march the legionary's burden was increased by his pack, which included his cooking utensils, mess kit, rations and spare clothing, carried in leather and string bags over the shoulder on a T-shaped pole, and weighing up to 13.6kg (29.9lb). Josephus indicates that the legionary would also carry all of his entrenching equipment if necessary. This included a pick, axe, saw, chain, leather strap, bill hook and a basket for shifting earth (Josephus, *Jewish War*, 3.93–96). It is no wonder that Julius Caesar ensured that a number of his legionaries were unencumbered by packs when on the march so that they could react rapidly to any attacks on the marching column (Caesar, *Gallic War*, 2.19; *African War*, 75).

We must marvel at the ability of the legionary to march long distances, with or without his pack, and then fight a battle. For example, six of the Vitellian legions that fought at the second battle of Cremona had marched 30 Roman

ABOVE LEFT **Imperial Gallic A helmet. The ridges broke the force of downward sword blows, deflecting them onto the broad neck guard. The ear holes allowed the legionary to hear commands; later models had curved guards above the ear holes. (Rijksmuseum, Nijmegen. Drawn by Steven D. P. Richardson after Robinson 1975, pl. 103)**

ABOVE RIGHT **Bronze Imperial Italic C helmet, probably lost at one of the battles of Cremona, AD 69. (Museo Stibbert, Florence. Drawn by Steven D. P. Richardson after Robinson 1975, pl. 155)**

Table showing weight of the fighting equipment bourne by an Augustan legionary.

	weight (kg)
Montefortino helmet	2
Mail shirt	12
Cross belts	1.2
Oval scutum	10
Mainz gladius and scabbard	2.2
Dagger and scabbard	1.1
Pilum	1.9
TOTAL	**30.4 (67lb)**

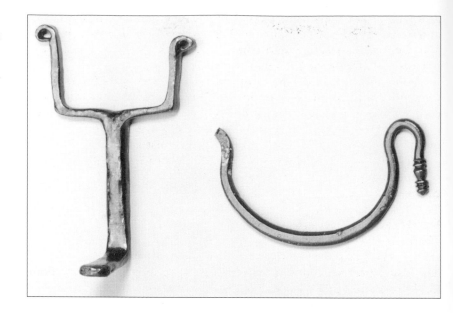

miles (*c.*27 miles) from Hostilia during the day, then fought throughout the night. Tacitus remarks that the battle would have gone their way if they had fed, warmed and rested themselves before falling upon the Flavian Army (*Histories*, 3.21–22). Ultimately the Vitellian legions' exhaustion caught up with them and they finally collapsed when they mistook legio III Gallica's customary hailing of the rising sun for the greeting of Flavian reinforcements (*ibid.*, 3.24). Exhaustion regularly figures in accounts of Roman battles which, as second Cremona illustrates, could go on for a considerable length of time. The burden of armour and the energy expended in wielding *pilum*, sword and shield put a limit on actual periods of combat and it is clear that battles were punctuated with regular lulls.

DAILY LIFE ON CAMPAIGN

Building camp

On campaign, battle was refused until a fortified camp was constructed. Pioneers, selected workmen from each century and military slaves, went ahead of the marching column clearing the way and making preparations for the construction of camp. Uneven ground was levelled and each unit knew its place, so construction proceeded in an orderly and swift manner. In peacetime *immunes* ('immune' from the dirty jobs) and *principales* (junior officers) enjoyed exemption from onerous building and cleaning details, but on campaign everyone had a function, whether as builder or guarding the construction from the enemy. Normally rectangular, the camp rampart was constructed from the turf and debris dug out from the perimeter ditch. Each wall had a gate large enough for draught animals to pass and from which emergency sallies could be made, and were protected by projecting sections of ditch and rampart. *Tribuli*, massive wooden caltrops, were placed along the ramparts and before the ditch. The ramparts also had towers and/or artillery emplacements. The interior of the camp was arranged around two main intersecting streets, with the headquarters and parade ground at the junction. Particular care was taken to provide adequate latrine trenches and a field hospital. Soldiers were quartered in rows of leather tents by unit and century.

Twenty per cent of the army was always on guard duty. The remainder had numerous duties to keep it busy: foraging, water collection (the proximity of water was essential for the route of the march and selection of the camp site), care of baggage animals, repair of equipment, cleaning duties, drill and administration. Sleeping and meals (breakfast and dinner) were at set times, and the regular routine of morning parade was maintained, when the daily watchword and duties were given.

Meals and entertainment

The main meal was taken in the evening, the only time when ordinary soldiers had free time. On campaign they carried rations for at least three days. At its most basic, this was hardtack or wheat for grinding into flour for bread, and bacon, cheese, oil/lard and *acetum* (cheap sour wine watered down for consumption). However, soldiers such as *sesquiplicarii* and *duplicarii*, those on pay-and-a-half and double pay, could afford to supplement their diet with good wine, beer and other foodstuffs, e.g. fish sauces, vegetables, preserved fruits. These could be bought from 'vendors' (*lixae*) following the army, really paramilitary plunderers licensed to raid enemy territory for the supply of the army and their own profit. Meat might become available to ordinary soldiers as a result of animal sacrifices for religious purposes on the march. When passing through provincial territory whole field armies might be freely fed and entertained by ultra-wealthy individuals seeking imperial favour, but generally this function was imposed on unfortunate communities.

Back at base, soldiers had access to bathhouses, where they could bathe, exercise, eat, drink and gamble. Settlements grew up around forts, providing shops, taverns and brothels. Legionary fortresses might also have amphitheatres for sporting and dramatic displays. It was not unknown for the suppliers of these entertainments to follow the army on campaign. Hunting was a favourite pastime for many soldiers and was permitted on campaign, but mainly for mounted officers and cavalry who justified it as training.

Camp followers

Many women accompanied marching armies, including the common-law wives of soldiers (Augustus banned soldiers from marrying) and prostitutes following individual units from base. Soldiers fathered children on campaign, but whether they or their mothers were accommodated in the camp is uncertain. Annexes built on to temporary camps could have been for their protection. In the 3rd century AD legionaries often rebelled when their families were put in danger. The number of women, children, *lixae* and servants following field armies normally exceeded the number of soldiers.

Striking camp

In the early morning, camp was struck as quickly and in as orderly a way as it had been constucted. The first trumpet call signalled the striking of the tents; the second to ready the pack animals and destroy the defenses; the third to fall into marching ranks. The troops were then asked three times by the commander's herald if they were ready for war? Each time they replied 'We are ready!', and the army departed (Polybius, 6.27–42; Josephus, *Jewish War*, 3.70–109).

BATTLE

Formations and depth of lines

The formation of the Roman Army that defeated Tacfarinas in AD 17 is typical: legio III Augusta in the centre flanked by 'light' auxiliary cohorts (presumably missile troops, though most cohorts were heavy infantry), with cavalry on the wings (Tacitus, *Annals*, 2.52). Such was the basic formation adopted in most battles (e.g. Mons Graupius) and is essentially that which Germanicus' marching column could have wheeled into at Idistaviso in AD 16 (Tacitus, *Annals*, 2.16–17), though this massive army would probably have deployed into two or more lines.

Multiple lines and reserves were usual in Roman battles. Caesar's regular use of the *triplex acies* (triple line), a 4-3-3 formation of cohorts (Caesar, *Civil War*, 1.83), is the most famous example of this. The first line of cohorts engaged the enemy while the second line would reinforce or replace it (if able); the third line could be used to build a camp, carry out flanking manoeuvres, reinforce the wings of the army or even split to form a fourth battle line.

We have evidence of Roman armies deploying in one, two, three, and occasionally in four battle lines. There is even a possibility of six lines if the six centuries of a cohort formed up one behind the other. Only when a cohort was isolated or operating alone as a *vexillatio* (combat detachment), might the centuries have formed into a number of lines and the cohort become a legion in miniature.

The depth of lines could be three, four, six, eight, ten or more ranks according to the circumstances, the effective strength of an army and its units and the experience of its men. In very close order the Roman Army probably fought in files, perhaps comprised of *contubernia*, but we have no explicit information about this. When in 'open' order the legionaries formed a kind of chessboard formation. This seems to have been the regular fighting order of the centuries because they did not rely on weight of formation to break through the enemy. Polybius indicates that each legionary occupied a space 1.8m across by 1.8m deep (18.28–30). Vegetius reduces the width to 90cm but increases the depth to 2m (*Epitome*, 3.14–15). The staggered formation and depth was necessary so that the *pilum* could be drawn back without injuring the man behind. Such staggered ranks are evident from representational evidence, for example the relief from the legionary *principia* at Mainz. Legionaries could adopt even looser formations appropriate to the enemy and terrain. Pompey's veteran legions fought in a particularly fluid open order after many years of fighting in Spain (Caesar, *Civil War*, 1.44).

Roman soldiers preferred to fight on open terrain, preferably dry and level, or on the crest of a slope because the enemy would have to advance up it and because it would offer momentum to charges (Caesar,

Gallic War, 1.25; Tacitus, *Annals*, 1.67–68). They did not like their formations to be too constricted by topography and preferred to have room in which to manoeuvre (Caesar, *Spanish War*, 30). If necessary, or if simply compelled, they would fight on narrower fronts, and deal with obstructions to the battle line, varying from trees to buildings as necessary, either reforming once around them or accepting that order was lost (Tacitus, *Annals*, 2.14; *Histories*, 2.41; Dio, 56.13.3–7).

Non-continuous battle lines

Roman battle lines were not continuous. Gaps in the line were essential for the cohesion and manoeuvrability of its component units. This is clear from the manipular legion. For example, at the Trebbia the Roman light troops retired through the gaps in the lines of the heavy infantry, and there is no suggestion that the lines closed up once they had passed and the battle proper began (Polybius, 3.73). Caesar indicates the existence of gaps in the line for the cohortal legion, when he states that two cohorts formed up with a small gap between them. The implication is not that small gaps were the norm, but that this gap was smaller than usual because the legionaries were unsure of British tactics (Caesar, *Gallic War*, 5.15). The sallies made by individual cohorts from a 'circular' *orbis* formation, suggests that there were gaps for the sake of cohesion even in such a defensive formation; the soldiers were aware that if they became a disorganised mass all would quickly be lost (Caesar, *Gallic War*, 5.34–35). The ready movement of officers through the battle lines also illustrates the existence of gaps (e.g. by Caesar, *ibid.*, 2.25).

The accounts of Polybius and Livy suggest that the gaps between the maniples were equal to the width of a maniple, to facilitate the rapid changing of the lines (Livy, 8.8; Polybius, 3.113, 15.9). Gaps equalling the frontage of a cohort seem too large, but might account for the rapid reinforcement or replacement of the first battle line by the third line as happened at Pharsalus (Caesar, *Civil War*, 3.94), but the centuries could have advanced through narrower gaps, one behind the other in column. We should also recall that gaps were present within the cohort itself – those between the centuries.

Worries about the potential problems of gaps in the line, namely that the enemy might 'pour through them', are negated when it is remembered that if an enemy army was to keep cohesion and not turn into a mass, it would also have gaps between its units. In any case, light troops covered the gaps in the lines and would attempt to catch the enemy in crossfire (Livy, 30.32; Herodian, 4.15.1).

Centurions, standard-bearers and *optiones* in battle

Centurions and standard-bearers

The centurion fought at the front, at the right of his century (Polybius, 6.24). He may have formed the extreme right of the first rank, but could actually have stood somewhat apart from the line and as a consequence be particularly exposed. It was not uncommon for all the centurions of a cohort to be killed in a single engagement, as occurred at the Sambre or second Cremona (Caesar, *Gallic War*, 2.25; Tacitus, *Histories*, 3.22).

The usual position of the standard-bearers was in front of the battle line. For example, when Suetonius Paulinus assaulted the Isle of Anglesey in AD 60, the Roman soldiers initially faltered at the sight of the Druids and wild women ranged before them but were spurred to action when the standard-bearers charged and led them forward (Tacitus, *Annals*, 14.30). Similarly, in a battle against Jugurtha, the legionaries of Metellus followed the standards (Sallust, *Jugurtha*, 51.1). Caesar ordered his legionaries not to advance more than four feet in front of the standards in a static formation at Ruspina in 47 BC, showing that his standard-bearers were in the front rank (Caesar, *African War*, 15). *Signiferi* also led the soldiers when on the march (Tacitus, *Annals*, 3.45). Thus if a column had to turn and form a line of battle the soldiers would follow the standards.

However, the existence of legionaries called *antesignani* (those who fought in front of the standards) indicates that *signiferi* were not always positioned at the front. *Antesignani* are usually identified as skirmishers who fought in front of the main battle line with light javelins and oval shields, but in some situations it is likely that standard-bearers were positioned behind the leading rank(s) of heavy infantry. In such cases the front rankers became *antesignani*: Vegetius refers to a standard battle line in which a rank of soldiers was positioned before the standard-bearers, and other soldiers surrounded them (*Epitome*, 2.15). *Signiferi* may have been withdrawn from the front because of their vulnerability, especially during prolonged battles, or in circumstances when the loss of standards was considered possible.

Leading the centuries in battle put standard-bearers in considerable danger, not least because they became a focus of attack for the enemy. Their casualty rates were as high as the centurions (Caesar, *Gallic War*, 2.25; Tacitus, *Histories*, 3.22). The loss of standards was a particular disgrace to the Romans, and their recovery was considered of critical importance. Augustus considered the return in 20 BC of the standards lost by Crassus and Antony to the Parthians as a particular diplomatic triumph (*Res Gestae*, 29). A primary objective of Germanicus in AD 14–15 was to recover the standards taken from Varus' army. He recaptured two eagles; the third was recovered in AD 41 (Tacitus, *Annals*, 1.60, 2.25, 41; Dio, 60.8.7). Thus, battles often deteriorated into numerous chaotic mêlées for possession of the standards, dramatically demonstrated at the first battle of Cremona:

> On Vitellius' side was the Twenty-first legion, entitled Rapax [*Rapacious*], long distinguished and renowned. On Otho's side was the First Adiutrix [*Helper*], which had never been in a battle before, but daring and eager for its first success. The First cut down the front ranks of the Twenty-First and captured their eagle. The shame of this so fired the Twenty-first that they charged the First, killed their legate, Orfidius Benignus, and captured many standards and *vexilla* [*flags*]. (Tacitus, *Histories*, 2.43).

Denarius of Augustus. A propaganda piece portraying the return in 20 BC of the Roman standards captured by the Parthians in 53 and 36 BC. (Hunter Coin Cabinet, University of Glasgow)

Victories could be measured not only by the number of casualties inflicted on the enemy but by the number of standards captured. Sulpicius Galba wrote to Cicero following the victory over Antony at Forum Gallorum in 43 BC, 'two eagles and sixty standards have been carried back – all Antony's! It has been a splendid achievement' (Cicero, *Ad Famliares*, 10.30).

Much of the legionary's morale was bound up in the standard of his century, for it was the totem that contained the *genius* or spirit of his sub-unit, and gave him a focus for direction in battle. Standards were objects of veneration, particularly the *aquila* (eagle) (Tertullian, *Apologeticus*, 16.8) and were kept in their own shrine at base, the *aedes principiorum*, a sacred place where fugitives might claim sanctuary (Tacitus, *Annals*, 1.39). Consequently, standard-bearers, especially

ABOVE LEFT **Gravestone of Cnaeus Musius, *aquilifer* of legio XIV Gemina. Pre-AD 43. (Landesmuseum, Mainz)**

ABOVE RIGHT **Gravestone of Luccius Faustus, *signifer* of legio XIV Gemina. His helmet is notable for its face mask. AD 70–92. (Landesmuseum, Mainz)**

eagle-bearers, were soldiers of influence, and it is no coincidence that it was to the senior *signiferi* that Germanicus leaked news of his advance on Xanten in AD 14, spurring the murder of the ringleaders of the legionary mutiny (Tacitus, *Annals*, 1.48).

Optiones

During Caesar's battle against the Belgae, frightened legionaries at the rear of the battle line peeled away from his hard-pressed centuries to avoid missiles (Caesar, *Gallic War*, 2.25). However, enough legionaries remained to hold the line. The containment of such a potentially disastrous disintegration of the century from the back was probably the primary duty of the *optio*. Polybius' description of the manipular legion notes that the two *optiones* of the maniple were normally found in the rear rank (6.24). Doubtless their function was the same as the rear-rankers of the hoplite phalanx. Xenophon recommended that the best fighters be positioned at the front and rear of the files in order that the less experienced hoplites would be led by the former and shoved along by the latter (Xenophon, *Memorabilia*, 3.1.8). During the late Republic or early Empire the *optio* seems actually to have stood a little behind the century. In numerous funerary sculptures he is represented with a long staff tipped with a ball-end. We know from the late Roman military handbook written by the Emperor Maurice that officers were positioned behind the battle line and used their spear-butts to prod soldiers back into line during combat (Maurice, *Strategikon*, 12.b.17; Speidel 1992: 24–26). This was surely the function of the *optio*'s staff. *Tesserarii* (officers of the watchword) are also represented with this type of staff and their function in battle should be considered similar to that of the *optiones*.

Vegetius emphasises that the first thing a recruit learned was to march in step at various speeds and maintain ranks, and that this became habitual through continuous practice (*Epitome*, 1.9). Although training and experience allowed legionaries to function in battle without orders (see Caesar, *Gallic War*, 2.20), in the confusion and extreme emotions of battle the soldier might not react as he did on the training ground. At Zama the Roman and Carthaginian infantry advanced on each other at a slow step; only when the two sides were within striking distance did the fore rank(s) of the Romans charge at the run (Polybius, 15.12). At the battle of Pharsalus, Caesar's army halted its advance on the Pompeians in order to gather its breath and redress its line (Caesar, *Civil War*, 3.93). There is no evidence for the legions using their trumpeters to sound marching tunes. The major function of the trumpeters was to sound and relay commands in battle (Vegetius, *Epitome*, 2.7, 22). Some commands may have signalled a particular marching pace (or formation). We can imagine the centurion or *signifer* maintaining the necessary pace with the Latin equivalent of 'Left! Right!', and the *optio* physically preventing any *milites* from falling out of step or dropping out of the formation. From depictions of the army on the march and soldiers in battle it seems that the leading leg was the left.

The importance of experience in battle

Experience in battle was crucial. When attacked on the River Sambre in 57 BC Caesar states that his soldiers, by their training and experience in previous battles, knew best what to do in response and were able to devise their own commands. What is more, the legionaries working on the camp did not waste time in trying to locate their particular cohorts or centuries but formed up behind the nearest standard (Caesar, *Gallic War*, 2.20–21; compare the disorganised Othonians at first Cremona – Tacitus, *Histories*, 2.41). Appian's account of the legio Martia and other veteran legions fighting at Forum Gallorum is also instructive. The legio Martia ordered the five cohorts of recruits accompanying it not to join in the fighting in case their inexperience caused confusion. Appian asserts that the experience of each veteran legionary 'made him his own commander' (Appian, *Civil Wars*, 3.67–68). At the battle fought outside Bonn between the Batavian cohorts and the remainder of legio I Germanica in AD 69, despite being outnumbered, the combat experience and skill of the Batavians prevailed (Tacitus, *Histories,* 4.20). Tacitus also indicates that each soldier knew his place so that formations could be drawn up quickly (*ibid.* 2.42).

The war cry
If time allowed before battle, the legions might draw lots for positions in the battle line (Tacitus, *Histories*, 2.41). The general would ride up and down the lines exhorting the individual units, and battle would begin when he ordered the army to advance. The trumpeters (*cornicines* and *bucinatores*) would then sound the signal and the soldiers would follow the standards forward.

The war cry was normally raised just before the *pila* were thrown and the legionaries charged (Caesar, *Gallic War*, 7.88; *Civil War*, 3.93). The war cry served to fortify the men delivering it and to frighten the enemy (Josephus, *Jewish War*, 3.259). However, Appian explains that the opposing veteran legions at Forum Gallorum raised no war cry because they knew it would not terrify their experienced opponents (Appian, *Civil War*, 3.68).

The charge and collision
Legionaries charged at close distance to the enemy. They had to get close enough to deliver an effective volley of *pila* (maximum range of 30m and preferably half that) but not so far as to exhaust the legionaries. Caesar's description of the opening of the battle of Pharsalus is instructive:

> Between the two lines there was only as much space left as was necessary for the charge of each army. But Pompey had previously ordered his men to await Caesar's attack without moving from their position, and to allow his line to fall into disorder. [He did this] in order that the first charge and impetus of the troops might be broken and their line spread out, and so the Pompeians marshalled in their proper ranks might attack a scattered enemy. He also hoped that the *pila* would fall with less effect if the men were kept in their place than if they themselves discharged *pila* and charged. Moreover, by having double the distance to run Caesar's soldiers would be breathless and exhausted …
>
> But when our soldiers, once the signal was given, had run forward with *pila* levelled and saw that the Pompeians were not advancing to meet them, profiting from the experience they had

gained in previous battles, they spontaneously checked their charge and halted about half-way, so that they would not approach the enemy with their energy wasted. After a short time, they renewed their rapid charge and threw their *pila* and quickly drew their swords. (Caesar, *Civil War*, 3.92–93)

On delivering the volley the fore rank charged. Only the legionaries in the front were close enough to the enemy to use their swords (Polybius, 18.30). Charging at the run with drawn swords, they sought to take advantage of the casualties caused by the *pila* and hack their way into the enemy formation before it regained order. Each legionary attempted to collide with an opponent, ramming his shield boss into belly or groin and pushing him over, while stabbing with the sword. Tacitus describes the hand-to-hand fighting between the Othonians and Vitellians at the first battle of Cremona:

> They struggled at close quarters, pressing with the weight of their bodies behind their shields. They threw no *pila* but crashed swords and axes through helmets and armour … [and were so close that] they could recognise one another. (*Histories*, 2.42)

The victims might fall backwards obstructing the men behind, causing further damage to the cohesion of their formation. The line of legionaries would exploit the gaps and cut their way deeper into the formation, hopefully causing the rear ranks to panic and peel away, resulting in the collapse of the formation.

The legionaries raised their shields and tucked their chins onto their chests to protect their faces and eyes not only from sword and spear blows but also from the danger of missiles. Thousands of catapult stones and bolts, sling bullets, arrows and a huge variety of spears and javelins were continuously flying through the air during battles. The prospect of imminent death or injury, as well as the noise of missiles cutting through the air and impacting, placed immense strain on the combatants, especially those in the rear ranks who were unable to fight, even to see what was happening at the front of the engaged line. When attacked by the Nervii in 57 BC, almost all the centurions and *signiferi* of legio XII were killed and Caesar describes how some of the rear-rankers were 'abandoning the fight, retiring to avoid the missiles' (Caesar, *Gallic War*, 2.25).

While the front rank was colliding with the enemy, the rear ranks followed up quickly and in orderly fashion, the legionaries banging their weapons against the back of their shields and yelling support to the swordsmen (Polybius, 15.12–13). They offered missile support, throwing their *pila* into the ranks of the enemy, and men in the second and third rank would take the place of any front-rank legionaries who fell. The presence of the rear ranks gave great moral support to the front-rank fighters, and acted as a physical and psychological deterrent to the enemy pressing forward against the thin line of swordsmen. Though the actual hand-to-hand fighting was limited to the first rank, if close enough the second rank might use their *pila* like thrusting spears (Plutarch, *Antony*, 45). The rear-rank legionaries were not supposed to press forward against the backs of their comrades (Polybius 18.30) because this might compromise the cohesion of the formation, toppling and trampling the soldiers at the front of files by the weight of men pushing from behind, as happened at Jerusalem in AD 70:

> The fallen were trampled down and crushed by the combatants. … Those in front had either to kill or be killed, there being no retreat. Those in the rear in either army pressed their comrades forwards leaving no intervening space between combatants. (Josephus, *Jewish War*, 6.76–78)

After the initial advance, the battle quickly settled into a number of local fights between sub-units positioned against each other. These individual units made rapid charges and fought the enemy hand-to-hand for a short time before withdrawing, drawing breath and resuming the fight at a longer range with missiles or charging again, perhaps adopting a different formation. Such fluidity of battle is emphasised by Tacitus' statement about the first battle of Cremona: 'the soldiers fought now hand-to-hand, again at a distance; they charged now in open order, again in close formation' (*Histories*, 2.42).

Sulpicius Galba, in a letter to Cicero, describes the fighting in one sector between the Caesarian factions at Forum Gallorum in 43 BC, and indicates the temporary nature of successful advances. Mounted on horseback, Galba had a superior view of the battlefield, but it made him a conspicuous target:

> When Antony's cavalry came in sight, neither the legio Martia nor the [two] praetorian cohorts could be held in check, and we began to follow their lead, being forced to do so, since we failed to keep them back. … We drew up a line of twelve cohorts. … Suddenly Antony brought his forces out of the village into line, and immediately charged. At first the battle could not have been more fiercely fought than it was on either side; although our right wing, where I was positioned with eight cohorts of the legio Martia, had at the first onset put to flight Antony's legio XXXV, so that our wing advanced more than 500 paces from its original position. Consequently, when the enemy's cavalry were attempting to outflank our wing, I began to retreat and sent my light-armed troops to oppose the Moorish cavalry, to prevent them attacking our soldiers in the rear. Meantime I became aware that I was surrounded by Antony's troops and that Antony himself was some distance behind me. In a moment I galloped up to the legion of recruits which was coming from the camp, slinging my shield behind me. The Antonians were close upon me, and our men were eager to hurl their *pila*. I was only saved by chance when my own men recognised me. (Cicero, *Ad familiares*, 10.30)

The battle swung in Antony's favour; the remaining cohorts of the legio Martia, the praetorian cohorts and legions of recruits were pushed back, but he failed to take the enemy camp. Retiring to his own camp he was surprised by two veteran legions under Aulus Hirtius and heavily defeated and lost two eagles. In this account of the second battle of Philippi (42 BC), between the forces of Brutus, assassin of Caesar, and the reconciled armies of Octavian and Antony, Appian describes the physical mechanics of such a defeat:

> There came a piercing shout [from the army of Antony and Octavian], the standards were raised on both sides, and the charge was violent and harsh. They had little need of volleys of arrows or stones or javelins … since they did not resort to the usual manoeuvres and tactics of battles, but, coming to close combat with drawn swords, inflicting and receiving thrusts, seeking to break each other's ranks. … The slaughter and groans were terrible. The bodies of the fallen were carried back and others stepped into their places from the reserves. The generals riding about and visible everywhere, urged the soldiers on in their charges, exhorted the toilers to toil on, to endure yet greater pressure, and relieved those who were exhausted so that there was always fresh courage at the front. Finally the soldiers of Octavian … pushed back the enemy's line as though they were turning around a very heavy machine. The latter were driven back step by step, slowly at first and without loss of courage. Presently their ranks broke and they retreated more rapidly, and then the second and third lines in the rear [i.e. *triplex acies* formation] retreated with them, all mingled together in disorder, crowded by each other and by the enemy, who pressed upon them without ceasing until it became plainly a flight. (Appian, *Civil Wars*, 4.128)

The battle fought at Bonn in AD 69, between over-confident legionaries of I Germanica and the rebel Batavian cohorts, illustrates victory over a

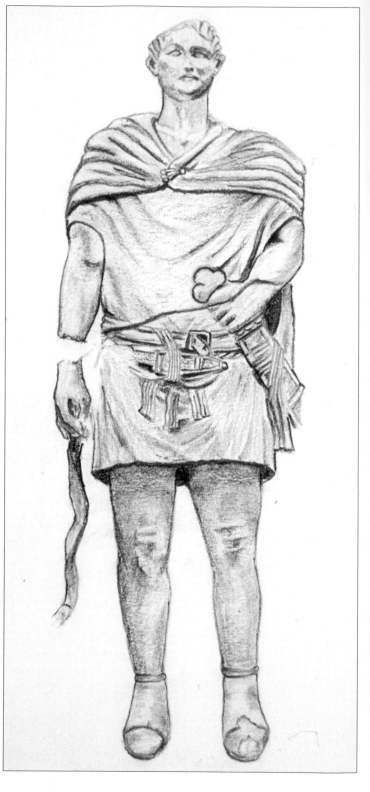

Gravestone of Minucius Lorarius ('the flogger'), centurion of *legio Martia*, c.49–42 BC. (Museo Civico, Padova. Drawn by Steven D. P. Richardson from Franzoni 1987, tav. XIII)

larger enemy through superior tactics and morale, and highlights the terrible aftermath of combat:

> [The Batavi envoy approaching the camp at Bonn] said that they were not making war on the Romans, on whose behalf they had often fought, but that they were weary of their long and profitless service and longed for home and a life of peace. If no one opposed them they would pass without doing any harm; but if armed resistance was offered, they would make a path with the sword. The legate hesitated but the soldiers pressed him to risk battle. He had 3,000 legionaries, some cohorts of Belgians which had been hastily raised, and a band of peasants and *lixae*, untrained but bold enough when they met actual danger. They immediately burst out of the gates to surround the numerically inferior Batavi. But they being veterans in arms, formed up into columns [*cunei*], with their ranks closed on every side, secure on front, flanks and rear, and they broke through the thin Roman line. When the Belgians gave way, the legionaries were driven back and in terror fled for the rampart and gates of the camp. Here were the greatest casualties, the ditches were heaped high with bodies and the Romans died not only by the sword and wounds, but as a result of the crush and many by their own weapons. (Tacitus, *Histories*, 4.20)

Rather than imagine the Batavi as smashing into or through the legionaries like a solid block, the *cuneus* should be viewed primarily as psychological. Roman soldiers certainly sought to use speed and weight to topple their opponents, but normally on a one-to-one basis, taking advantage of the chaos caused to the enemy by a missile volley. The advance of the massed *cuneus* formation towards a single, narrow part of the line was unnerving, if not terrifying, for the limited number of soldiers having to meet its attack, especially if they were inexperienced. It was also disconcerting for those watching from other parts of the line, who might worry what their chances of survival were if that section of the line was compromised.

Bonn also illustrates that the real casualties in Roman battles were inflicted during the pursuit of broken troops, who, with their backs turned and often trying to rid themselves of cumbersome equipment, were unable to defend themselves. The Batavi left dead legionaries and auxiliaries clogging the ditches around the legionary fortress and, in their panic, the Romans were the victims of their own weapons, perhaps accidentally in the chaotic crush of those trying to enter the fortress gate, but perhaps also by soldiers trying to cut a way to safety through other fugitives.

Lulls during battle

Despite what happened at Bonn, charges were rarely decisive at the first attempt, and armies, or sections of opposing battle lines, would gradually fall back and separate during the course of a battle. The first battle of Cremona was clearly punctuated by lulls with the lines falling apart and then charging again (Tacitus, *Histories*, 2.41–44). Of the battle of Forum Gallorum Appian says that 'when they were tired, they [the legionaries] separated for a brief time to recover as if they were engaged in training exercise, and then attacked each other again' (*Civil Wars*, 3.68). Polybius confirms that such 'breaks' were normal when he remarks that the fighting at Cannae was unusual because once the two sides had engaged they remained locked in combat (3.115). It can only have been during such lulls that exhausted fighters were replaced with fresh soldiers (Caesar, *Gallic War*, 7.85; *Civil War*, 3.94), or the wounded carried back from the line (Polybius 15.14). At such times men took the opportunity to eat and especially drink (Plutarch, *Crassus*, 23), dehydration being a particular danger to men fighting in heavy armour, often in the summer months.

Caesar indicates how close the opposing battle lines could be during such lulls. His legionaries were so close to Ariovistus' Germans during a lull that they had no time to throw their *pila* (maximum range of 30m) to meet a sudden charge of the Germans (*Gallic War*, 1.52). Such lulls help account for the length of battles, which could range from three or four hours (the average for smaller late-Roman armies according to Vegetius, *Epitome*, 3.9), to day-long affairs, sometimes resuming the following day or even continuing into the night (e.g. second Cremona). Conversely, a smaller battle such as that fought between the legionaries and Batavians at Bonn in AD 69 was probably over within minutes.

After the battle

Roman commanders were well aware of the lure of booty, and in their pre-battle exhortations, besides the usual reminders of past victories and the justice of their cause, they readily emphasised the riches to be won. Cicero thought that Mark Antony's legionaries were entirely motivated by the prospect of enrichment (*Philippics*, 8.9). Corbulo and Suetonius Paulinus stressed the prospect of booty if the legions were successful in battle (Tacitus, *Annals*, 13.39, 14.36). Plundering enemy camps and stripping the dead was one of the first acts after victory in battle, or during a lull (Tacitus relates the infamous case of Julius Mansuetus who was killed and plundered by his own son at second Cremona; *Histories*, 3.25).

Next, the victorious might erect a trophy made of arms taken from the enemy (Tacitus, *Annals*, 2.18, 22). In extreme circumstances enemy corpses and heads taken during battle might be used to adorn such trophies, as occurred after Caesar's troops defeated the Pompeians outside Munda:

> Shields and *pila* taken from among the enemy's arms were placed to serve as a palisade, corpses as a rampart. On top, impaled on sword points, were severed human heads. ('Caesar', *Spanish War*, 32)

The Roman wounded would be treated during and after the battle by competent *medici* (surgeons and orderlies), but the chances of surviving a major wound were not high in this pre-antibiotic era (see Salazar 2000). Those who survived injuries but were unfit for further service would be granted *missio causaria* – a medical discharge. This meant that a soldier would receive the same privileges as a veteran who had received *honesta missio* (honourable discharge), i.e. superior legal status to civilians, exemption from taxes and civic duties.

Aureus of Claudius, AD 41–45, showing a trophy of captured German arms commemorating the victories of his father Drusus in 16–9 BC. (Hunter Coin Cabinet, University of Glasgow)

The number of Roman and perhaps enemy casualties would be recorded. Josephus' figures for Roman and Jewish casualties in the Jewish War seem accurate, and might have been derived from official Roman records. The Roman dead were to be buried (Appian, *Civil Wars*, 1.43). It was a disgrace to leave Roman soldiers unburied (Tacitus, *Annals*, 4.73). Captives taken during the battle might be executed or mutilated, but more often they were sold as slaves (Tacitus, *Annals*, 13.39). The ancient economy was founded on slavery and it was for this purpose that paramilitary slavers and freebooters known as *lixae* followed the army (Feig Vishnia 2002). Other captives were retained for eventual triumphal processions and probable execution in Rome.

Let us end our discussion with Vegetius' distillation of, and Josephus' conclusion on, the Roman military ethos. They indicate why the Romans usually won, and how, when they lost, they would strive to erase the memory of defeat by careful planning, training and pure tenacity:

He who desires peace, let him prepare for war. He who wants victory, let him train soldiers diligently. He who wishes a successful outcome, let him fight with strategy, not at random. No one dares challenge or harm one who he realises will win if he fights. (Vegetius, *Epitome* 3, preface).

It is no wonder that this vast empire of theirs has come to them as a prize of valour, not of Fortune. (Josephus, *Jewish War*, 3.72)

WEBSITES

For the Varian disaster and finds from Kalkriese, visit the excellent website of
Varusschlacht im Osnabrücker Land – Museum und Park Kalkriese:
www.kalkriese-varusschlacht.de

The most extensive collection of relevant finds in the UK is to be found in the
British Museum in London: www.thebritishmuseum.ac.uk

The Hunterian Museum at the University of Glasgow has considerable numismatic
material relating to our period, as well as an important collection of
2nd-century Roman military equipment: www.hunterian.gla.ac.uk

Armamentarium, run under the auspices of the University of Newcastle, is a site
dedicated to Roman arms and armour and contains the best guide to museums
across Europe with relevant material: www.ncl.ac.uk/archive/arma

Those wishing to find out more about re-enactors, displays and the reconstruction
of equipment are advised to visit the sites of:

The Ermine Street Guard: www.esg.ndirect.co.uk

Legio X Gemina: www.gemina.nl

The most useful on-line bibliography of the armies of Greece and Rome is Hugh
Elton's Warfare in the Ancient World: www.fiu.edu/~eltonh/army.html

Gary Brueggeman's website is excellent for those wishing to investigate Roman
tactics and fighting styles: www.geocities.com/Athens/Oracle/6622/

GLOSSARY

Acies battle line/formation (*duplex* – double; *triplex* – triple)
Antesignani those who fought in front of the standards
Aquila eagle standard of the legion
Aquilifer eagle-bearer
Balteus military belt (sometimes called a *cingulum*); identifies a soldier
Caligae military boots; identifies a soldier
Caligati soldiers; those serving in military boots, including centurions, and inferior in status to equestrians and sentors
Castra fort or camp
Centurion (centurio) commander of the century
Century (centuria) sub-unit of the legion comprising 80 soldiers, 60 per legion
Cohort (cohors) formation of six centuries/three maniples, ten per legion
Commanipularis/manipularis fellow soldier in the same maniple; term of comradeship
Commilito fellow soldier; expression of comradeship, applied across the board from ordinary soldiers to generals and the emperor
Contubernalis tent-/mess-mate; term of comradeship, affection
Contubernium sub-unit of the century comprised of eight men who shared a room/tent, ten per century
Dilectus levy, conscription
Dolabra military pick-axe
Duplicarius soldier receiving double pay, e.g. *optio, signifer*
Equestrian Order later Republican and Imperial Rome's 'middle' or business class, originally signifying men whose wealth was sufficient to equip themselves as cavalrymen. Equestrians were superior in class to ordinary soldiers (*caligati*), hence they could be promoted directly to centurionates (and higher ranks) without prior experience
Exercitus the army
Expediti lightly equipped soldiers
Frater brother; used as term of comradeship, affection
Gladius sword
Hastatus 'spear-armed'; centurial title
Immunes legionaries exempt from menial duties
Legate (legatus) senatorial commander of the legion
Legio legion, chief formation of the Roman Army, comprised of 60 centuries organised in ten cohorts
Lixae paramilitary slavers who helped supply the army on campaign
Lorica armour; *hamata* – mail; *squamata* – scale; *segmentata* – articulated

Maniple (*manipulus*) 'handful'; paired centuries, *prior* and *posterior*

Medici generic term for medical staff including high-ranking doctors and junior orderlies

Miles soldier

Natalis aquilae birthday of the eagle/foundation of legion celebration

Optio centurion's deputy, one per century

Orbis enclosed defensive formation, sometimes circular or semi-circular

Origo place of origin

Pilum legionary javelin

Pilus 'spear/javelin-armed'; centurial title

Posterior 'rear'; centurial title

Postsignani those who fought behind the standards

Praefectus equestrian commander of legions in Egypt

Praefectus castrorum camp prefect, third-in-command of legion

Praemia discharge bonus/pension

Primi ordines front/first rankers; centurions of first cohort

Primus pilus 'first spear' or *pilum*; leading centurion of the first cohort and most senior in the legion

Principales under and junior officers including the *tesserarius*, *optio* and *signifer*

Princeps 'foremost'; centurial title

Prior 'front'; centurial title

Pugio dagger

Scutum curved legionary shield

Senatorial Order/Senate Ruling class and council of Rome, comprised of annually elected magistrates, chiefly consuls, praetors, aediles and tribunes, and ex-magistrates, who directed or advised on Roman policy

Sesquiplicarius soldier receiving pay-and-a-half, e.g. *tesserarius*

Signifer standard-bearer, one per century

Signum standard

Stipendium year of (paid) service; annual salary

Tesserarius officer of the watch, one per century

Testudo 'tortoise'; entirely enclosed formation with roof and wall of shields

Tribuli wooden caltrops used to defend camps

Tribune (*tribunus*) legionary officer; six per legion, five equestrian, one senatorial acting as aides to legate

Vexillarius bearer of the flag standard of a legionary detachment (vexillatio) or the corps of veterans attached to a legion (vexillum veteranorum)

Vexillatio vexillation; detachment from a legion or cohort

Vexillum flag standard of a detachment

Vexillum veteranorum unit of veterans attached to the legion, approximately 500 strong with its own command and administrative structure (13 BC until c.mid-1st century AD)

Vitis the vine wood staff of the centurion, indicative of his rank

BIBLIOGRAPHY

Alston, R. A., 1994: 'Roman military pay from Caesar to Diocletian', *Journal of Roman Studies* 84, 113–123

Bishop, M. C. and Coulston, J. N. C., 1993: *Roman Military Equipment from the Punic Wars to the Fall of Rome* (London)

Brunt, P. A., 1974: 'Conscription and Volunteering in the Roman Imperial Army', *Scripta Classica Israelica* 1, 90–115, in Brunt 1990: *Roman Imperial Themes*, 188–214, with addenda on 512–15

Connolly, P., 1981: *Greece and Rome at War* (London)

Connolly, P., 1991: 'The Roman Fighting Technique Deduced from Armour and Weaponry', in Maxfield and Dobson (eds) 1991: *Roman Frontier Studies* 1989 (Exeter), 358–63

Connolly, P., 1997: '*Pilum, gladius* and *pugio* in the Late Republic', *JRMES* 7, 41–57

Deschler-Erb, E., 2000: 'Nielierung auf Buntmetall: Ein Phänomen der frühen römischen Kaiserzeit', *Kölner Jahrbuch* 33, 383–96

Feig Vishnia, R., 2002: 'The Shadow Army – The Lixae and the Roman Legions', *Zeitschrift für Papyrologie* 139, 265–72

Franzius, G., 1995: 'Die Römischen Funde aus Kalkriese 1987–95', *JRMES* 6, 69–88

Franzoni, C., 1987: *Habitus atque habitudo militis. Monumenti funerari di militari nella Cisalpina romana* (Roma)

Fuentes, N., 1987: 'The Roman Military Tunic', in M. Dawson (ed), 1987: *Roman Military Equipment: The Accoutrements of War*, Proceedings of the Third Roman Military Equipment Research Seminar, [BAR 336], 41–75

Gilliver, C.H., 1993: 'Hedgehogs, Caltrops and Palisade Stakes', *JRMES* 4, 49–54

Goldsworthy, A. K., 1996: *The Roman Army at War, 100 BC–AD 200* (Oxford)

ILS – H. Dessau (ed), *Inscriptiones Latinae Selectae* (Berlin, 1892–1916)

Isaac, B., 1994: 'Hierarchy and Command-Structure in the Roman Army', in Y. Le Bohec (ed), 1994: *La Hiérarchie (Rangordnung) de l'armée romaine* (Paris), 23–31

Junkelmann, M., 1986: *Die Legionen des Augustus* (Mainz)

Keppie, L. J. F., 1984: *The Making of the Roman Army: From Republic to Empire* (London)

Keppie, L. J. F., 1997: 'The changing face of the Roman legions', *Papers of the British School at*

Rome 65, 89–102, in Keppie 2000: 50–63

Keppie, L. J. F., 2000: *Legions and Veterans: Roman Army Papers 1971–2000*, Mavors 12 (Stuttgart)

Maxfield, V. A., 1981: *The Military Decorations of the Roman Army* (London)

Milner, N. P., 1996: *Vegetius: Epitome of Military Science*, 2nd ed. (Liverpool)

Robinson, H. R., 1975:, *The Armour of Imperial Rome* (London)

Roth, J., 1994: 'The Size and Organisation of the Roman Imperial Legion', *Historia* 43, 346–362

Salazer, C. F., 2000: *The Treatment of War Wounds in Graeco-Roman Antiquity* (Leiden)

Scheidel, W., 1996: 'Measuring Age, Sex and Death in the Roman Empire', *Journal of Roman Archaeology*, supplement 21 (Ann Arbor)

Schlüter, W, 1999: *The Battle of the Teutoburg Forest* in J.D. Wilson & R.J.A. Wilson (eds.), 1999: 'Roman Germany: Studies in Cultural Interaction' (Journal of Roman Archaeology Supplementary Series no.32), 125-59

Speidel, M. P., 1992: *The Framework of an Imperial Legion* (Caerleon)

Sumner, G., 2002: *Roman Military Clothing* (1) (Oxford)

Ulbert, G., 1969: 'Gladii aus Pompeji. Vorarbeiten zu einem Corpus römischer Gladii', *Germania* 47, 97–128

COLOUR PLATE COMMENTARY

A: VETERAN OF LEGIO XII ANTIQUA, 32–31 BC

The inevitable war between Antony and Octavian began in 32 BC. Antony moved west to defend Greece and Macedonia but found his fleet blockaded in the Gulf of Ambracia by Agrippa. His land army of 19 legions was cut off by Octavian on the promontory of Actium, at the mouth of the Gulf. On 2 September 31 BC, Antony and Cleopatra fought their way free of the blockade but most of their fleet was destroyed during the battle. The fleet was manned by four legions, and 5,000 legionaries died in the battle. The surviving ships surrendered and the land army went over to Octavian (Plutarch, *Antony*, 60–68). Having fled to Egypt, Antony despaired and took his own life, leaving Octavian in control of the whole Empire.

The plate proposes that legio XII Antiqua was one of the legions of the fleet, and shows a veteran marine. The legion was retained by Octavian as XII Fulminata.

The legionary is loosely modelled after the funerary portrait of Publius Gessius, a probable Caesarian legionary (Keppie 1984: 226). His mail shirt and Montefortino C helmet **(1)**, with glued-in felt lining, follow equipment worn by legionaries depicted on the Altar of Domitius Ahenobarbus, perhaps mid-1st century BC. The bronze belt fittings come from Delos, c.75 BC, the *gladius Hispaniensis* from Berry-Bouy, c.20 BC. The dagger derives from the examples excavated from Alesia (52 BC) and Oberaden. The sword details illustrate the alternate parallel **(2a)** and waist **(2b)** forms of the blade. The scabbard follows an Augustan find from Dangstetten in Germany. The mail detail **(3)** illustrates the method of construction, one riveted ring linking four welded rings. The triple-ply *scutum* **(4)** is the 1st-century BC example from Fayum in Egypt. The detail **(4a)** illustrates the lamination of the planed strips of wood and the felt and leather facings. The blue colour of the shield, tunic and helmet plume was recommended for marines by Vegetius (*Epitome*, 4.37). The ship's prow emblem follows the denarius struck in the legion's honour by Antony. Legio XI Fretensis had a similar emblem, they having fought for Octavian against the fleet of Sextus Pompeius.

The *pila* **(5)** have heavy shanks after examples from Valencia and Alesia (70s and 52 BC); the method of shank attachment **(5a)** follows the finds from the Augustan fortress of Oberaden in Germany.

B: LEGIONARY PRESS-GANG IN OSTIA, PORT OF ROME, AD 6–9

The recently conquered territories of Pannonia and Dalmatia rose in revolt in AD 6. The Romans were diverted from an invasion of Bohemia and found themselves fighting auxiliaries formerly in their service. Casualties were high and it took three years to quell the revolt. The manpower crisis escalated when

Mark Antony 'legionary' denarius, 32–31 BC, honouring a *cohors speculatorum*, a cohort of bodyguards and scouts. *Speculatores* were incorporated into the Imperial legions and Praetorian Guard. The ships' prows on the standards suggest marine service. (Hunter Coin Cabinet, University of Glasgow)

three legions were destroyed in Germany in AD 9. Augustus resorted to levying recruits in Rome and the surrounding area. Few men came forward voluntarily and the emperor began seizing property, removing citizenship and resorting ultimately to executions. Men were chosen by lot to serve, many considerably older than the usual ages of recruits (Dio, 56.23; Tacitus, *Annals*, 1.31). The plate illustrates one such unfortunate civilian, beaten unconscious by the soldiers (Apulieus, *Metamorphoses*, 7.4, 9.39). In the background legionaries are pelted with roof tiles and pottery.

The equipment of the centurion **(1)** follows a belt and dagger from Velsen in Holland and the *gladius* from Rheingönheim in Germany with its silver-plated hilt. His staff (*vitis*) and the way he wears his sword on the left, indicate his rank. The ordinary legionary **(2)** carries a *fustis* (military club) and a curved rectangular *scutum*; this form of the shield was in use by c.10 BC. The *optio* **(3)** is identified by his knobbed staff and he wears a *paenula*, the standard heavy cloak of the soldier until the late 2nd century AD. The embossed and decorated belt fittings of the legionary and *optio* indicate that such expensive equipment was not limited to officers (Tacitus, *Histories*, 1.57).

C: *CONTUBERNIUM* ON THE MARCH, POST-AD 14

The plate depicts a file of eight legionaries in marching order. They wear *paenulae*, the typical heavy-duty cloak of the legionary. Leather covers protect their curved rectangular and oval shields. They are carried via a harness system **(1)** devised by Marcus Junkelmann and used with success in his practical experiments, but the harness remains hypothetical (Junkelmann 1986: 176–79). The legionaries' helmets, a mixture of Montefortino, Coolus and Imperial Gallic patterns, are slung over their chests in a fashion known from provincial and state monuments.

Other kit, comprising a leather stuff-bag and net bag (for personal effects and rations), pot, pan and water bottle, is slung from T-shaped poles. Their tent and heavy equipment, such as entrenching tools – axe, pick-axe, spade, turf cutter – are carried by the mules (see background), but on campaign soldiers might carry everything except the heaviest items such as quern stones for grinding grain into flour. The general Marius was famous for cutting down the baggage accompanying armies, forcing legionaries to carry all their equipment, hence their nickname of 'Marius' mules' (Frontinus, *Stratagems*, 4.1.7). The muleteers are military slaves (*calones*).

D: LEGIONARY FIGHTING TECHNIQUES

1 illustrates a typical heavy-armed legionary of the first half of the 1st century AD throwing his heavy *pilum* prior to charging with his sword. The legionaries relied on the shock and confusion caused by the *pila* volley to maximise their own rapid sword charge, when each legionary would aim to collide with an opponent and stab him as he fell back (see Plate F).

2 and **3** show two different kinds of legionary fighting *expediti*, without body armour. 2 illustrates a dedicated light-armed legionary. His flat oval shield is more manoeuvrable than the regular *scutum*, and his light javelins allow him to fight in advance of the battle line (*antesignani*) or deliver missile support over the heads of his comrades (following Mainz *principia* relief). In battles characterised by missile duels such legionaries would have dominated the fighting.

3 shows a regular legionary advancing without armour. Caesar, Tacitus and Dio all refer to heavy infantry relieved of their body armour to increase their speed and manoeuvrability in battle.

4 shows an Augustan legionary in a crouch stance advocated by Connolly (1991). He suggests that this was a standard fighting position, but Goldsworthy believes it to be

Adze-hammer from Kalkriese, AD 9. (Varusschlacht im Osnabrücker Land, Museum und Park Kalkriese)

impractical, as it negates the protection of the shield, places great strain on the left arm and exposes the back and shoulders (1996: 173). However, it should be considered an option for a legionary wishing to get under the guard of an opponent armed with a slashing sword.

E: MARCHING CAMP, 1ST CENTURY AD

Marching camps were fundamental to Roman military practice (Plutarch, *Pyrrhus*, 16), giving armies on the march a secure campsite each night, as well as a position to retire to if a battle was unsuccessful. The general Corbulo declared that wars were really won with the pick-axe (*dolabra*) (Frontinus, *Stratagems*, 4.7.2), and camp-building techniques were easily transferred to siege warfare, in which the Romans excelled.

The illustration shows the waterproof goatskin tents of a century that are visible behind the rampart. Tents would normally be further back, out of missile range. Each *contubernium* of eight legionaries shared a small cramped tent, but the centurion had a large tent to himself, the standard of the century set before it (see **1** for a typical row). It is uncertain if the *signifer* and *optio* had separate tents. Most of the legionaries are engaged in the clearing of the ditch and lashing together of palisade stakes to form massive caltrops (*tribuli*) (convincingly proposed by Gilliver, 1993). The rampart itself has been faced with sods of turf. The workers' exposed tunics reveal a knot of material at the back of the neck; if loosened the neck slit was wide enough to pass an arm through and allow the wearing of the tunic over just one shoulder, as often occurred in hot conditions. Fully armed legionaries guard the construction, and at least 20 per cent of the army would have been on guard duty at any time, perhaps 50 per cent in the face of the enemy. The gates of the camp (at the centre of each wall, were particularly heavily guarded, normally with projecting sections of ditch and rampart to split any force that attempted to assault it. The gates opened onto the two main intersecting streets of the camp that led to the headquarters, market place and drill ground.

F: BATTLE OF THE TEUTOBURG FOREST, GERMANY, AUTUMN AD 9

Marcus Caelius (**1**), a leading centurion of legio XVIII, leads a small band of veterans and *calones* (army slaves) against

Military pick-axe (*dolabra*) lost in the Varian disaster, AD 9. (Varusschlacht im Osnabrücker Land, Museum und Park Kalkriese)

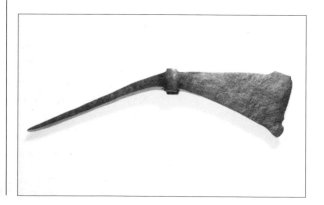

Arminius' Cherusci during the three-day battle in which three legions (XVII, XVIII, XIX) and nine auxiliary regiments were destroyed.

Quinctilius Varus (not shown), acting on the information of Arminius, the trusted Cherusci war chief and former auxiliary officer, led a Roman Army in autumn AD 9 to contain a rebellion in partially subdued territory. Expecting to rendezvous with levies from the Chersuci, Varus was himself led into an ambush prepared by Arminius in the Teutoburg forest. Constrained by wooded hills to the left, marshes to the right and turf walls to the front, the Roman Army sustained the initial attack, but having been marching through 'friendly' territory it was strung out and disorderly and ultimately unable to extricate itself. The continual hit-and-run attacks of the Chersuci increased disorder and panic, and only a few soldiers survived to return across the River Rhine (Dio, 56.18–22; Velleius Paterculus, 2.117–120). The site of the battle was recently located at Kalkriese, near Osnabrück (Schlüter 1999).

All the equipment illustrated is derived from finds from Kalkriese, predominantly from fragments of helmets, armour, shields, swords, pila, belt fittings and entrenching equipment (Franzius 1995).

Caelius' mail shirt and decorations of *armillae, torques, phalerae* and civic crown follows the portrait on his gravestone from Xanten in Holland. Decorations were worn in battle (Caesar, *Spanish War*, 23), but it is uncertain whether the fragile oak-leaf crown was worn in action. The transverse crest and silvered greaves indicate his rank (Vegetius, *Epitome*, 2.13). His helmet is an Imperial Gallic D, normally dated to the second quarter of the 1st century. Fragments of Imperial Gallic helmets have been discovered at Kalkriese, and other finds there, such as the *lorica segmentata* worn by the veteran to Caelius' left (**2**), indicate that many patterns of equipment had come into service earlier than previously supposed. He also wears an Imperial Gallic helmet, but an early pattern from the late first century BC. The veteran (**4**) illustrates the more traditional image of the Augustan legionary equipped with mail armour, with bronze securing hooks and a bronze Coolus helmet and curve-sided *scutum*.

The silver face mask worn beneath the helmet of the *vexillarius* (**3**), the flag-bearer of legio XVIII's veterans, is one of the most spectacular finds from Kalkriese. The mask may actually have belonged to the helmet of an auxiliary cavalryman but legionary standard-bearers certainly wore such mask-helmets during the 1st century AD. The pick-axe (*dolabra*) wielded by the *calo* (**4**) was certainly used in battle by legionaries (Tacitus, *Annals*, 3.46; *Histories*, 2.42), and military slaves would be equipped with such items in their probable camp-building function (Josephus, *Jewish War*, 3.69–70, 78).

G: PRIOR CENTURY IN BATTLE, 1ST CENTURY AD

Here we see a *prior* (front) century formed in four ranks of 20, with the centurion, identified by his transverse helmet crest, positioned on the extreme right of front rank (**1**). The *signifer* (standard-bearer [**2**]) is at the centre of the formation to prevent him from being killed during the first clash and stop the standard from falling into enemy hands (Vegetius, *Epitome*, 2.15), but standard-bearers regularly fought in the front rank. Not illustrated here, but a *posterior* (rear) century

Helmet face mask of silver, edged with bronze from Kalkriese, AD 9. (Varusschlacht im Osnabrücker Land, Museum und Park Kalkriese)

Aureus of Claudius, AD 46–7, illustrating the triumphal arch built to celebrate his conquest of southern Britain in AD 43. (Hunter Coin Cabinet, University of Glasgow)

would be drawing up behind, preparing to throw light-socketed *pila* over the heads of the leading century (Arrian, *Ectaxis contra Alanos*, 15–16), and light-armed troops would cover the gaps between the centuries, aiming to catch any enemy who tried to exploit the gaps in the line in a vicious crossfire of javelins.

The inset reveals the regular 'chessboard' formation of the legionaries. Having advanced within range of the enemy the front ranks have thrown their lead-weighted *pila* and are charging at the run with drawn swords. The standard-bearer has withdrawn into the centre of the third rank and will follow up with the remainder of the century once they have delivered their *pila*. The three figures positioned behind the century are the *optio* (centurion's deputy, **[3]**), *cornicen* (trumpeter, **[4]**) and *tesserarius* (watchword officer, **[5]**). The *optio* and *tesserarius* are positioned to use their long staffs to shove legionaries back into line and prevent any attempt by the rear rankers to flee. The *cornicen* (also withdrawn to the rear following the initial advance because of his essential command function) relays the commands given by the general's trumpeters to the *signifer*; the soldiers might not be able to hear the trumpet commands and follow the directions of the standard.

H: LEGIONARY OF II AUGUSTA, BRITAIN AD 43

Claudius unexpectedly became emperor in AD 41 when his nephew Caligula was assassinated. Needing military success to consolidate his position, he embarked on the conquest of southern Britain in AD 43, an enterprise originally planned by his predecessor. The invasion force was composed of four legions (certainly II Augusta, XIV Gemina, and perhaps IX Hispana and legio XX) and auxiliary

forces. Advancing rapidly, the Roman forces won a major victory outside Camulodunum (Colchester) and the emperor entered the tribal capital in triumph on an elephant.

Legio II Augusta was under the command of Vespasian during the invasion. It fought in 30 engagements and captured 20 hill forts (Suetonius, *Vespasian*, 4). Here we see a legionary re-equipped for the expedition, but many would have been equipped similarly to their late Republican predecessors with bronze helmets, mail armour and curve-sided scuta.

His curved rectangular *scutum* **(1)** was probably more widespread now but not the standard pattern. Similarly, his Corbridge A-type cuirass (armour) of *lorica segmentata*, so dominant on Trajan's column, might have been limited to specialist fighters. His helmet is a high-quality Imperial Gallic F, but figure **2** is a contemporary Imperial Italic C in bronze, worn by many legionaries but of inferior construction.

The lead-weighted *pilum* **(3)** follows a representation on a panel surviving from the Arch of Claudius in Rome, built to celebrate the conquest (Koeppel 1983). Such weighted *pila* may have been introduced during the reign of Tiberius. The newly introduced 'Pompeii' *gladius* **(4)**, a true short sword with a short point and parallel edged blade, was used alongside the older Mainz-type patterns **(5)**. The famous Mainz-type *gladius* **(6)**, with Romulus, Remus and she-wolf embossed scabbard, found in the Thames at Fulham, almost dates to the conquest period. (Ulbert 1969). The dagger **(7)** is worn at an angle, following the fashion of its Spanish antecedents.

The *caligae* nailing patterns **(8)** follow examples from Kalkriese and Hod Hill, illustrating the similarity to modern shoe soles. The openwork pattern of the upper, cut from a single piece of leather, is also illustrated **(9)**.

INDEX

References to illustrations are shown in **bold**. Plates are shown with page and caption locators in brackets.

Actium, battle of 60
Anglesey, Isle of 47-48
Antony, Mark 4, 53-54, 60
Appian 18, 51, 54, 55-56
armour 31-32, **F2**(38, 62), 41
  see also cuirasses; helmets
armour, mail **A3**(33, 60), **41**
Augustus, Emperor (previously Octavian) 4, 7, 12, 13, 60, 61

Batavi 54-55, 56
battle, after the 56-57
battle, experience in 50-51
battle, lulls during 55-56
battle charge and collision 51-55
battle lines 46-47
belts, military (*baltei*) 23-24, **24**
Billienus Actiacus, Marcus 20, **21**
Bonn 54-55, 56
boots (*caligae*) 23, 24, **H8, H9**(40, 63)
bravado 22-23
Britain 47-48, 63

Caecina, Aulus, and his army 13-14
Caelius, Marcus **15, F**(38, 62)
Caesar, Julius 4, 10, 22-23, 43, 51-52
camp, marching **E**(37, 62), 44-46
centuries 7-9, **G**(39, 62-63)
centurions 7-8, 14, **B1**(34, 61), **G1**(39, 62), 47, **54**
centurions' deputies (*optiones*) **B3**(34, 61), **G3**(39, 63), 50
Claudius 63
clothing 24, **25**, 25, **B3**(34, 61), **C**(35, 61)
cohorts 7, 8, 9
coins **4, 7, 10, 16, 19, 27, 48, 57, 60, 63**
comradeship 17-18
conscription 10-11, **B**(34, 60-61)
contubernium **C**(35, 61), **E**(37, 62)
Cordus, Flavoleius **31**
Cremona, battles of 23, 43-44, 48, 51, 52, 53, 55
cuirasses 31-32, **32, H1**(40, 63)
  see also armour

Decrius 16

entertainment 45
equipment, burden of 43-44

Faustus, Luccius **49**

fighting techniques **D**(36, 61-62)
formations 11-12, **G**(39, 62), 46
Forum Gallorum 49, 51, 53, 55-56

Galba, Sulpicius 49, 53
Gamala, siege of 23
gravestones **15, 21, 31, 49, 54**
group identity 17-19
  see also contubernium

helmets **A1**(33, 60), **C**(35, 61), **F**(38, 62), **H1, H2**(40, 63), 41-43, **42, 43, 44, 63**

initiative 22-23

Jerusalem, siege of 18-19, 53
Josephus 21, 53, 57

Laetus, Suetonius 19
legionaries **31, 32, B2**(34, 61), **D1, D4**(36, 61-62), **E**(37, 62), **H1**(40, 63), **41**
  lightly-armed (*expediti*) **26**, 31, **D2, D3**(36, 61-62)
legions 6-9, 16-17
  I Germanica 51, 54-55
  III Cyrenaica 11
  III Gallica 44
  V Alaudae 10, 19, 22
  XII Antiqua **A1**(33, 60), 52
  XIV Gemina **31, 49**
  XV Apollinaris 23
  XVIII **F**(38, 62)
  XXII Deiotariana, Galatian 10, 11
  XXXV 53
  Augustan 16, **H1**(40, 63), 46
  Martian 17, 18, 51, 53, **54**
  Pannonian 15
  Vitellian 23, 43-44, 48
Lorarius, Minucius **54**
Lucilius 15

Mainz *principia* relief **26, 31**, 31, **32, 41**
Marius 61
meals 45
Mons Graupius 27, 28, 43
Munda 22, 56
Musius, Cnaeus **49**

Nervii 22-23, 52
Numonius, Vala 15

oath, military 19-20
Octavian (later Emperor Augustus) 4, 7, 12, 13, 60, 61

officers, senior 8
Ostia, port of Rome **B**(34, 60-61)
Otho 15-16, 19

Paterculus, Velleius 14-15
Paulinius, Suetonius 23, 47-48
Percennius 15
Pharsalus, battle of 50, 51-52
Philippi, battle of 53-54
Pompey 51
Pullo, Titus 22-23

recruits 9-10
rewards 20-22
Rufus, Aufidienus 15
Rufus, Marcus Helvius 20

scabbards **28, 29**, 29-30, **30, H4, H6**(40, 63)
shields (*scuta*) **27**, 27, **A4**(33, 60), **B2**(34, 61), **C**(35, 61), **D**(36, 61-62), **H1**(40, 63)
skirmishers (*antesignani*) **D2**(36, 61), 48
standard-bearers 7, 8, **32, F3**(38, 62), **G2**(39, 62-63), 47-48, **49**, 49-50
standards **48**, 48, 49

Tacfarinas 16, 20, 46
Tacitus 8, 9, 13-14, 15-16, 21-22, 48, 52, 55
Teutoburg Forest, battle of the 14-15, **F**(38, 62)
Tiberius, Emperor 10, 20
Titus 21
tools **F4**(38, 62), **61, 62**
trumpeters (*cornicines*) 7, **G4**(39, 63), 50, 51

unit identity 16-17

Varus, Quinctilius, and his army 14-15, **F**(38, 62)
Vegetius 9, 11, 19-20, 57
veterans 7, 10-11, 12-13, **A1**(33, 60), **F2, F4**(38, 62)
Vitellius 21-22
Vorenus, Lucius 22-23

war cry 51
watchword officers (*tesserarii*) 7, **G5**(39, 63), 50
weapons
  club (*fustis*) **B2**(34, 61)
  daggers (*pugio*) 30, **H7**(40, 63)
  javelins (*pila*) **25**, 25-26, **26, A5**(33, 60), **D1**(36, 61-62), **H3**(40, 63)
  swords (*gladii*) **28**, 28-30, **29, A2**(33,